I Ching
Book of Changes

Graphics by Greg C. Grace

ISBN: 1-84013-474-7

Copyright © Axiom Publishing 2001

This edition produced for Grange Books
Units 1-6 Kingsnorth Ind. Est.
Hoo, nr Rochester
Kent ME3 9ND
United Kingdom
www.Grangebooks.co.uk

Grange Books PLC

I CHING

BOOK OF CHANGES

translated by Richard Wilhelm

CONTENTS

Foreword
by Carl Gustav Jung

Since I am not a sinologue, a foreword to the Book of Changes from my hand must be a testimonial of my individual experience with this great and singular book. It also affords me a welcome opportunity to pay tribute again to the memory of my late friend, Richard Wilhelm. He himself was profoundly aware of the cultural significance of his translation of the I Ching, a version unrivaled in the West.

If the meaning of the Book of Changes were easy to grasp, the work would need no foreword. But this is far from being the case, for there is so much that is obscure about it that Western scholars have tended to dispose of it as a collection of "magic spells," either too abstruse to be intelligible, or of no value whatsoever. Legge's translation of the I Ching, up to now the only version available in English, has done little to make the work accessible to Western minds. Wilhelm, however, has made every effort to open the way to an understanding of the symbolism of the text. He was in a position to do this because he himself was taught the philosophy and the use of the I Ching by the venerable sage Lao Nai-hsüan; moreover, he had over a period of many years put the peculiar technique of the oracle into practice. His grasp of the living meaning of the text gives his version of the I Ching a depth of perspective that an exclusively academic knowledge of Chinese philosophy could never provide.

I am greatly indebted to Wilhelm for the light he has thrown upon the complicated problem of the I Ching, and for insight as regards its practical application as well. For more than thirty years I have interested myself in this oracle technique, or method of exploring the unconscious, for it has seemed to me of uncommon significance. I was already fairly familiar with the I Ching when I first met Wilhelm in the early nineteen twenties; he confirmed for me then what I already knew, and taught me many things more.

I do not know Chinese and have never been in China. I can assure my reader that it is not altogether easy to find the right access to this monument of Chinese thought, which departs so completely from our ways of thinking. In order to understand what such a book is all about, it is imperative to cast off certain prejudices of the Western mind. it is a curious fact that such a gifted and intelligent people as the Chinese has never developed what we call science. Our science, however, is based upon the principle of causality, and causality is considered to be an axiomatic truth. But a great change in our standpoint is setting in. What Kant's Critique of Pure Reason failed to do, is being accomplished by modern physics. The axioms of causality are being shaken to their foundations: we know now that what we term natural laws are merely statistical truths and thus must necessarily allow for exceptions. We have not sufficiently taken into account as yet that we need the laboratory with its incisive restrictions in order to demonstrate the invariable validity of natural law. If we leave things to nature, we see a very different picture: every process is partially or totally interfered with by chance, so much so that under natural circumstances a course of events absolutely conforming to specific laws is almost an exception.

The Chinese mind, as I see it at work in the I Ching, seems to be exclusively preoccupied with the chance aspect of events. What we call coincidence seems to be the chief concern of this peculiar mind, and what we worship as causality passes almost unnoticed. We must admit that there is something to be said for the immense importance of chance. An incalculable amount of human effort is directed to combating and restricting the nuisance or danger represented by chance. Theoretical considerations of cause and effect often look pale and dusty in comparison to the practical results of chance. It is all very well to say that the crystal of quartz is a hexagonal prism. The statement is quite true in so far as an ideal crystal is envisaged. But in nature one finds no two crystals exactly alike, although all are unmistakably hexagonal. The actual form, however, seems to appeal more to the Chinese sage than the ideal one. The jumble of natural laws constituting empirical reality holds more significance for him than a causal explanation of events that, moreover, must usually be separated from one another in order to be properly dealt with The manner in which the I Ching tends to look upon reality seems to disfavor our causalistic procedures. The moment under actual observation appears to the ancient Chinese view more of a chance hit than a clearly defined result of concurring causal chain processes. The matter of interest seems to be the configuration formed by chance events in the moment of observation, and not at all the hypothetical reasons that seemingly account for the coincidence. While the Western mind carefully sifts, weighs, selects, classifies, isolates, the Chinese picture of the moment encompasses everything down to the minutest nonsensical detail, because all of the ingredients make up the observed moment.

Thus it happens that when one throws the three coins, or counts through the forty-nine yarrow stalks, these chance details enter into the picture of the moment of observation and form a part of it — a part that is insignificant to us, yet most meaningful to the Chinese mind. With us it would be a banal and almost meaningless statement (at least on the face of it) to say that whatever happens in a given moment possesses inevitably the quality peculiar to that moment. This is not an abstract argument but a very practical one. There are certain connoisseurs who can tell you merely from the appearance, taste, and behavior of a wine the site of its vineyard and the year of its origin. There are antiquarians who with almost uncanny accuracy will name the time and place of origin and the maker of an objet d'art or piece of furniture on merely looking at it. And there are even astrologers who can tell you, without any previous knowledge of your nativity, what the position of sun and moon was and what zodiacal sign rose above the horizon in the moment of your birth. In the face of such facts, it must be admitted that moments can leave long-lasting traces.

In other words, whoever invented the I Ching was convinced that the hexagram worked out in a certain moment coincided with the latter in quality no less than in time. To him the hexagram was the exponent of the moment in which it was cast — even more so than the hours of the clock or the divisions of the calendar could be — inasmuch as the hexagram was understood to be an indicator of the essential situation prevailing in the moment of its origin.

This assumption involves a certain curious principle that I have termed synchronicity, a concept that formulates a point of view diametrically opposed to that of causality. Since the latter is a merely statistical truth and not absolute, it is a sort of working hypothesis of how events evolve one out of another, whereas synchronicity takes the coincidence of events in space and time as meaning something more than mere chance, namely, a peculiar interdependence of objective events among themselves as well as with the subjective (psychic) states of the observer or observers.

The ancient Chinese mind contemplates the cosmos in a way comparable to that of the modern physicist, who cannot deny that his model of the world is a decidedly psychophysical structure. The microphysical event includes the observer just as much as the reality underlying the I Ching comprises subjective, i.e., psychic conditions in the totality of the momentary situation.

Just as causality describes the sequence of events, so synchronicity to the Chinese mind deals with the coincidence of events. The causal point of view tells us a dramatic story about how D came into existence: it took its origin from C, which existed before D, and C in its turn had a father, B, etc. The synchronistic view on the other hand tries to produce an equally meaningful picture of coincidence. How does it happen that A', B', C', D', etc., appear all in the same moment and in the same place? It happens in the first place because the physical events A' and B' are of the same quality as the psychic events C' and D', and further because all are the exponents of one and the same momentary situation. The situation is assumed to represent a legible or understandable picture.

Now the sixty-four hexagrams of the I Ching are the instrument by which the meaning of sixty-four different yet typical situations can be determined. These interpretations are equivalent to causal explanations. Causal connection is statistically necessary and can therefore be subjected to experiment. Inasmuch as situations are unique and cannot be repeated, experimenting with synchronicity seems to be impossible under ordinary conditions. In the I Ching, the only criterion of the validity of synchronicity is the observer's opinion that the text of the hexagram amounts to a true rendering of his psychic condition. It is assumed that the fall of the coins or the result of the division of the bundle of yarrow stalks is what it necessarily must be in a given "situation," inasmuch as anything happening in that moment belongs to it as an indispensable part of the picture. If a handful of matches is thrown to the floor, they form the pattern characteristic of that moment. But such an obvious truth as this reveals its meaningful nature only if it is possible to read the pattern and to verify its interpretation, partly by the observer's knowledge of the subjective and objective situation, partly by the character of subsequent events. It is obviously not a procedure that appeals to a critical mind used to experimental verification of facts or to factual evidence. But for someone who likes to look at the world at the angle from which ancient China saw it, the I Ching may have some attraction.

My argument as outlined above has of course never entered a Chinese mind. On the contrary, according to the old tradition, it is "spiritual agencies," acting in a mysterious way, that make the yarrow stalks give a meaningful answer. These powers form, as it were, the living soul of the book. As the latter is thus a sort of animated being, the tradition assumes that one can put questions to the I Ching and expect to receive intelligent answers.

Thus it occurred to me that it might interest the uninitiated reader to see the I Ching at work. For this purpose I made an experiment strictly in accordance with the Chinese conception: I personified the book in a sense, asking its judgment about its present situation, i.e., my intention to present it to the Western mind.

Although this procedure is well within the premises of Taoist philosophy, it appears exceedingly odd to us. However, not even the strangeness of insane delusions or of primitive superstition has ever shocked me. I have always tried to remain unbiased and curious — rerum novarum cupidus. Why not venture a dialogue with an ancient book that purports to be animated? There can be no harm in it, and the reader may watch a psychological procedure that has been carried out time and again throughout the millennia of Chinese civilization, representing to a Confucius or a Lao-tse both a supreme expression of spiritual authority and a philosophical enigma. I made use of the coin method, and the answer obtained was hexagram 50, Ting, THE CALDRON.

In accordance with the way my question was phrased, the text of the hexagram must be regarded as though the I Ching itself were the speaking person. Thus it describes itself as a caldron, that is, as a ritual vessel containing cooked food. Here the food is to be understood as spiritual nourishment. Wilhelm says about this:
The ting, as a utensil pertaining to a refined civilization, suggests the fostering and nourishing of able men, which redounded to the benefit of the state. . . .Here we see civilization as it reaches its culmination in religion. The ting serves in offering sacrifice to God. . . .The supreme revelation of God appears in prophets and holy men. To venerate them is true veneration of God. The will of God, as revealed through them, should he accepted in humility.

Keeping to our hypothesis, we must conclude that the I Ching is here testifying concerning itself.

When any of the lines of a given hexagram have the value of six or nine, it means that they are specially emphasized and hence important in the interpretation. In my hexagram the "spiritual agencies" have given the emphasis of a nine to the lines in the second and in the third place.

The text says:
Nine in the second place means:
There is food in the ting.
My comrades are envious,
But they cannot harm me.
Good fortune.

Thus the I Ching says of itself: "I contain (spiritual) nourishment." Since a share in something great always arouses envy, the chorus of the envious is part of the picture. The envious want to rob the I Ching of its great possession, that is, they seek to rob it of meaning, or to destroy its meaning. But their enmity is in vain. Its richness of meaning is assured; that is, it is convinced of its positive achievements, which no one can take away.

The text continues:
Nine in the third place means:
The handle of the ting is altered.
One is impeded in his way of life.
The fat of the pheasant is not eaten.
Once rain falls, remorse is spent.
Good fortune comes in the end.

The handle [German Griff] is the part by which the ting can be grasped [gegriffen]. Thus it signifies the concept (Begriff) one has of the I Ching (the ting). In the course of time this concept has apparently changed, so that today we can no longer grasp (begreifen) the I Ching. Thus "one is impeded in his way of life." We are no longer supported by the wise counsel and deep insight of the oracle; therefore we no longer find our way through the mazes of fate and the obscurities of our own natures. The fat of the pheasant, that is, the best and richest part of a good dish, is no longer eaten. But when the thirsty earth finally receives rain again, that is, when this state of want has been overcome, "remorse," that is, sorrow over the loss of wisdom, is ended, and then comes the longed-for opportunity. Wilhelm comments: "This describes a man who, in a highly evolved civilization, finds himself in a place where no one notices or recognizes him. This is a severe block to his effectiveness." The I Ching is complaining, as it were, that its excellent qualities go unrecognized and hence lie fallow. It comforts itself with the hope that it is about to regain recognition.

The answer given in these two salient lines to the question I put to the I Ching requires no particular subtlety of interpretation, no artifices, no unusual knowledge. Anyone with a little common sense can understand the meaning of the answer; it is the answer of one who has a good opinion of himself, but whose value is neither generally recognized nor even widely known. The answering subject has an interesting notion of itself: it looks upon itself as a vessel in which sacrificial offerings are brought to the gods, ritual food for their nourishment. It conceives of itself as a cult utensil serving to provide spiritual nourishment for the unconscious elements or forces ("spiritual agencies") that have been projected as gods — in other words, to give these forces the attention they need in order to play their part in the life of the individual. Indeed, this is the original meaning of the word religio — a careful observation and taking account of (from relegere the numinous.

The method of the I Ching does indeed take into account the hidden individual quality in things and men, and in one's own unconscious self as well. I have questioned the I Ching as one questions a person whom one is about to introduce to friends: one asks whether or not it will be agreeable to him. In answer the I Ching tells me of its religious significance, of the fact that at present it is unknown and misjudged, of its hope of being restored to a place of honor — this last obviously with a sidelong glance at my as yet unwritten foreword, and above all at the English translation. This seems a perfectly understandable reaction, such as one could expect also from a person in a similar situation.

But how has this reaction come about? Because I threw three small coins into the air and let them fall, roll, and come to rest, heads up or tails up as the case might be. This odd fact that a reaction that makes sense arises out of a technique seemingly excluding all sense from the outset, is the great achievement of the I Ching. The instance I have just given is not unique; meaningful answers are the rule. Western sinologues and distinguished Chinese scholars have been at pains to inform me that the I Ching is a collection of obsolete "magic spells." In the course of these conversations my informant has sometimes admitted having consulted the oracle through a fortune teller, usually a Taoist priest. This could be "only nonsense" of course. But oddly enough, the answer received apparently coincided with the questioner's psychological blind spot remarkably well.

I agree with Western thinking that any number of answers to my question were possible, and I certainly cannot assert that another answer would not have been equally significant. However, the answer received was the first and only one; we know nothing of other possible answers. It pleased and satisfied me. To ask the same question a second time would have been tactless and so I did not do it: "the master speaks but once." The heavy-handed pedagogic approach that attempts to fit irrational phenomena into a preconceived rational pattern is anathema to me. Indeed, such things as this answer should remain as they were when they first emerged to view, for only then do we know what nature does when left to herself undisturbed by the meddlesomeness of man. One ought not to go to cadavers to study life. Moreover, a repetition of the experiment is impossible, for the simple reason that the original situation cannot be reconstructed. Therefore in each instance there is only a first and single answer.

To return to the hexagram itself. There is nothing strange in the fact that all of Ting, THE CALDRON, amplifies the themes announced by the two salient lines. The first line of the hexagram says:
A ting with legs upturned.
Furthers removal of stagnating stuff.
One takes a concubine for the sake of her son.
No blame.

A ting that is turned upside down is not in use. Hence the I Ching is like an unused caldron. Turning it over serves to remove stagnating matter, as the line says. Just as a man takes a concubine when his wife has no son, so the I Ching is called upon when one sees no other way out. Despite the quasi-legal status of the concubine in China, she is in reality only a somewhat awkward makeshift so likewise the magic procedure of the oracle is an expedient that may be utilized for a higher purpose. There is no blame, although it is an exceptional recourse.

The second and third lines have already been discussed.
The fourth line says:
The legs of the ting are broken.
The prince's meal is spilled
And his person is soiled.
Misfortune.

Here the ting has been put to use, but evidently in a very clumsy manner, that is, the oracle has been abused or misinterpreted. In this way the divine food is lost, and one puts oneself to shame. Legge translates as follows: "Its subject will be made to blush for shame." Abuse of a cult utensil such as the ting (i.e., the I Ching) is a gross profanation. The I Ching is evidently insisting here on its dignity as a ritual vessel and protesting against being profanely used.

The fifth line says:

The ting has yellow handles, golden carrying rings. Perseverance furthers.

The I Ching has, it seems, met with a new, correct (yellow) understanding, that is, a new concept (Begriff) by which it can be grasped. This concept is valuable (golden). There is indeed a new edition in English, making the book more accessible to the Western world than before.

The sixth line says:

The ting has rings of jade.

Great good fortune.

Nothing that would not act to further.

Jade is distinguished for its beauty and soft sheen. If the carrying rings are of jade, the whole vessel is enhanced in beauty, honor, and value. The I Ching expresses itself here as being not only well satisfied but indeed very optimistic. One can only await further events and in the meantime remain content with the pleasant conclusion that the I Ching approves of the new edition.

I have shown in this example as objectively as I can how the oracle proceeds in a given case. Of course the procedure varies somewhat according to the way the question is put. If for instance a person finds himself in a confusing situation, he may himself appear in the oracle as the speaker. Or, if the question concerns a relationship with another person, that person may appear as the speaker. However, the identity of the speaker does not depend entirely on the manner in which the question is phrased, inasmuch as our relations with our fellow beings are not always determined by the latter. Very often our relations depend almost exclusively on our own attitudes, though we maybe quite unaware of this fact. Hence, if an individual is unconscious of his role in a relationship, there may be a surprise in store for him; contrary to expectation, he himself may appear as the chief agent, as is sometimes unmistakably indicated by the text. It may also occur that we take a situation too seriously and consider it extremely important, whereas the answer we get on consulting the I Ching draws attention to some unsuspected other aspect implicit in the question.

Such instances might at first lead one to think that the oracle is fallacious. Confucius is said to have received only one inappropriate answer, i.e., hexagram 22, GRACE — a thoroughly aesthetic hexagram. This is reminiscent of the advice given to Socrates by his daemon— "You ought to make more music"— whereupon Socrates took to playing the flute. Confucius and Socrates compete for first place as far as reasonableness and a pedagogic attitude to life are concerned; but it is unlikely that either of them occupied himself with "lending grace to the beard on his chin," as the second line of this hexagram advises. Unfortunately, reason and pedagogy often lack charm and grace, and so the oracle may not have been wrong after all.

To come back once more to our hexagram. Though the I Ching not only seems to be satisfied with its new edition, but even expresses emphatic optimism, this still does not foretell anything about the effect it will have on the public it is intended to reach. Since we have in our hexagram two yang lines stressed by the numerical value nine, we are in a position to find out what sort of prognosis the I Ching makes for itself. Lines designated by a six or a nine have, according to the ancient conception, an inner tension so great as to cause them to change into their opposites, that is, yang into yin, and vice versa. Through this change we obtain in the present instance hexagram 55, Chin, PROGRESS.

The subject of this hexagram is someone who meets with all sorts of vicissitudes of fortune in his climb upward, and the text describes how he should behave. The I Ching is in this same situation: it rises like the sun and declares itself, but it is rebuffed and finds no confidence — it is "progressing, but in sorrow." However, "one obtains great happiness from one's ancestress." Psychology can help us to elucidate this obscure passage. In dreams and fairy tales the grandmother, or ancestress, often represents the unconscious, because the latter in a man contains the feminine component of the psyche. If the I Ching is not accepted by the conscious, at least the unconscious meets it halfway, and the I Ching is more closely connected with the unconscious than with the rational attitude of consciousness. Since the unconscious is often represented in dreams by a feminine figure, this may be the explanation here. The feminine person might be the translator, who has given the book her maternal care, and this might easily appear to the I Ching as a "great happiness." It anticipates general understanding, but is afraid of misuse —"Progress like a hamster." But it is mindful of the admonition, "Take not gain and loss to heart." It remains free of "partisan motives." It does not thrust itself on anyone.

The I Ching therefore faces its future on the American book market calmly and expresses itself here just about as any reasonable person would in regard to the fate of so controversial a work. This prediction is so very reasonable and full of common sense that it would be hard to think of a more fitting answer.

All of this happened before I had written the foregoing paragraphs. When I reached this point, I wished to know the attitude of the I Ching to the new situation. The state of things had been altered by what I had written, inasmuch as I myself had now entered upon the scene, and I therefore expected to hear something referring to my own action. I must confess that I had not been feeling too happy in the course of writing this foreword, for, as a person with a sense of responsibility toward science, I am not in the habit of asserting something I cannot prove or at least present as acceptable to reason. It is a dubious task indeed to try to introduce to a critical modern public a collection of archaic "magic spells," with the idea of making them more or less acceptable. I have undertaken it because I myself think that there is more to the ancient Chinese way of thinking than meets the eye. But it is embarrassing to me that I must appeal to the good will and imagination of the reader, inasmuch as I have to take him into the obscurity of an age-old magic ritual. Unfortunately I am only too well aware of the arguments that can be brought against it. We are not even certain that the ship that is to carry us over the unknown seas has not sprung a leak somewhere. May not the old text be corrupt? Is Wilhelm's translation accurate? Are we not self-deluded in our explanations?

The I Ching insists upon self-knowledge throughout. The method by which this is to be achieved is open to every kind of misuse, and is therefore not for the frivolous-minded and immature; nor is it for intellectualists and rationalists. It is appropriate only for thoughtful and reflective people who like to think about what they do and what happens to them — a predilection not to be confused with the morbid brooding of the hypochondriac. As I have indicated above, I have no answer to the multitude of problems that arise when we seek to harmonize the oracle of the I Ching with our accepted scientific canons. But needless to say, nothing "occult" is to be inferred. My position in these matters is pragmatic, and the great disciplines that have taught me the practical usefulness of this viewpoint are psychotherapy and medical psychology. Probably in no other field do we have to reckon with so many unknown quantities, and nowhere else do we become more accustomed to adopting methods that work even though for a long time we may not know why they work. Unexpected cures may arise from questionable therapies and unexpected failures from allegedly reliable methods. In the exploration of the unconscious we come upon very strange things, from which a rationalist turns away with horror, claiming afterward that he did not see anything. The irrational fullness of life has taught me never to discard anything, even when it goes against all our theories (so short-lived at best) or otherwise admits of no immediate explanation. It is of course disquieting, and one is not certain whether the compass is pointing true or not; but security, certitude, and peace do not lead to discoveries. It is the same with this Chinese mode of divination. Clearly the method aims at self-knowledge, though at all times it has also been put to superstitious use.

I of course am thoroughly convinced of the value of self-knowledge, but is there any use in recommending such insight, when the wisest of men throughout the ages have preached the need of it without success? Even to the most biased eye it is obvious that this book represents one long admonition to careful scrutiny of one's own character, attitude, and motives. This attitude appeals to me and has induced me to undertake the foreword. Only once before have I expressed myself in regard to the problem of the I Ching: this was in a memorial address in tribute to Richard Willielm. For the rest I have maintained a discreet silence. It is by no means easy to feel one's way into such a remote and mysterious mentality as that underlying the I Ching. One cannot easily disregard such great minds as Confucius and Lao-tse, if one is at all able to appreciate the quality of the thoughts they represent; much less can one overlook the fact that the I Ching was their main source of inspiration. I know that previously I would not have dared to express myself so explicitly about so uncertain a matter. I can take this risk because I am now in my eighth decade, and the changing opinions of men scarcely impress me any more; the thoughts of the old masters are of greater value to me than the philosophical prejudices of the Western mind.

I do not like to burden my reader with these personal considerations; but, as already indicated, one's own personality is very often implicated in the answer of the oracle. Indeed, in formulating my question I even invited the oracle to comment directly on my action. The answer was hexagram 29, K'an, THE ABYSMAL. Special emphasis is given to the third place by the fact that the line is designated by a six.

This line says:

Forward and backward, abyss on abyss.
In danger like this, pause at first and wait,
Otherwise you will fall into a pit in the abyss.
Do not act in this way.

Formerly I would have accepted unconditionally the advice, "Do not act in this way," and would have refused to give my opinion of the I Ching, for the sole reason that I had none. But now the counsel may serve as an example of the way in which the I Ching functions. It is a fact that if one begins to think about it, the problems of the I Ching do represent "abyss on abyss," and unavoidably one must "pause at first and wait" in the midst of the dangers of limitless and uncritical speculation; otherwise one really will lose his way in the darkness. Could there be a more uncomfortable position intellectually than that of floating in the thin air of unproved possibilities, not knowing whether what one sees is truth or illusion? This is the dreamlike atmosphere of the I Ching, and in it one has nothing to rely upon except one's own so fallible subjective judgment. I cannot but admit that this line represents very appropriately the feelings with which I wrote the foregoing passages. Equally fitting is the comforting beginning of this hexagram —"If you are sincere, you have success in your heart" — for it indicates that the decisive thing here is not the outer danger but the subjective condition, that is, whether one believes oneself to be "sincere" or not.

The hexagram compares the dynamic action in this situation to the behavior of flowing water, which is not afraid of any dangerous place but plunges over cliffs and fills up the pits that lie in its course (K'an also stands for water). This is the way in which the "superior man" acts and "carries on the business of teaching."

K'an is definitely one of the less agreeable hexagrams. It describes a situation in which the subject seems in grave danger of being caught in all sorts of pitfalls. Just as in interpreting a dream one must follow the dream text with utmost exactitude, so in consulting the oracle one must hold in mind the form of the question put, for this sets a definite limit to the interpretation of the answer. The first line of the hexagram notes the presence of the danger: "In the abyss one falls into a pit." The second line does the same, then adds the counsel: "One should strive to attain small things only." I apparently anticipated this advice by limiting myself in this foreword to a demonstration of how the I Ching functions in the Chinese mind, and by renouncing the more ambitious project of writing a psychological commentary on the whole book.

The fourth line says:

A jug of wine, a bowl of rice with it;

Earthen vessels

Simply handed in through the window.

There is certainly no blame in this.

Wilhelm makes the following comment here:

Although as a rule it is customary for an official to present certain introductory gifts and recommendations before he is appointed, here everything is simplified to the utmost. The gifts are insignificant, there is no one to sponsor him, he introduces himself; yet all this need not be humiliating if only there is the honest intention of mutual help in danger.

Wilhelm makes the following comment here:

Although as a rule it is customary for an official to present certain introductory gifts and recommendations before he is appointed, here everything is simplified to the utmost. The gifts are insignificant, there is no one to sponsor him, he introduces himself; yet all this need not be humiliating if only there is the honest intention of mutual help in danger.

It looks as if the book were to some degree the subject of this line.

The fifth line continues the theme of limitation. If one studies the nature of water, one sees that it fills a pit only to the rim and then flows on. It does not stay caught there:

The abyss is not filled to overflowing,

It is filled only to the rim.

But if, tempted by the danger, and just because of the uncertainty, one were to insist on forcing conviction by special efforts, such as elaborate commentaries and the like, one would only be mired in the difficulty, which the top line describes very accurately as a tied-up and caged-in condition.

Indeed, the last line often shows the consequences that result when one does not take the meaning of the hexagram to heart.

In our hexagram we have a six in the third place. This yin line of mounting tension changes into a yang line and thus produces a new hexagram showing a new possibility or tendency. We now have hexagram 48, Ching, THE WELL. The water hole no longer means danger, however, but rather something beneficial, a well:
Thus the superior man encourages the people at their work,
And exhorts them to help one another.

The image of people helping one another would seem to refer to the reconstruction of the well, for it is broken down and full of mud. Not even animals drink from it. There are fishes living in it, and one can shoot these, but the well is not used for drinking, that is, for human needs. This description is reminiscent of the overturned and unused ting that is to receive a new handle. Moreover, this well, like the ting, is cleaned. But no one drinks from it:
This is my heart's sorrow,
For one might draw from it.

The dangerous water hole or abyss pointed to the I Ching, and so does the well, but the latter has a positive meaning: it contains the waters of life. It should he restored to use. But one has no concept (Begriff) of it, no utensil with which to carry the water; the jug is broken and leaks. The ting needs new handles and carrying rings by which to grasp it, and so also the well must be newly lined, for it contains "a clear, cold spring from which one can drink." One may draw water from it, because "it is dependable."

It is clear that in this prognosis the speaking subject is again the I Ching, representing itself as a spring of living water. The preceding hexagram described in detail the danger confronting the person who accidentally falls into the pit within the abyss. He must work his way out of it, in order to discover that it is an old, ruined well, buried in mud, but capable of being restored to use again.
I submitted two questions to the method of chance represented by the coin oracle, the second question being put after I had written my analysis of the answer to the first. The first question was directed, as it were, to the I Ching: what had it to say about my intention to write a foreword? The

second question concerned my own action, or rather the situation in which I was the acting subject who had discussed the first hexagram. To the first question the I Ching replied by comparing itself to a caldron, a ritual vessel in need of renovation, a vessel that was finding only doubtful favor with the public. To the second question the reply was that I had fallen into a difficulty, for the I Ching represented a deep and dangerous water hole in which one might easily be mired. However, the water hole proved to be an old well that needed only to be renovated in order to be put to useful purposes once more.

These four hexagrams are in the main consistent as regards theme (vessel, pit, well); and as regards intellectual content they seem to be meaningful. Had a human being made such replies, I should, as a psychiatrist, have had to pronounce him of sound mind, at least on the basis of the material presented. Indeed, I should not have been able to discover anything delirious, idiotic, or schizophrenic in the four answers. In view of the I Ching's extreme age and its Chinese origin, I cannot consider its archaic, symbolic, and flowery language abnormal. On the contrary, I should have had to congratulate this hypothetical person on the extent of his insight into my unexpressed state of doubt. On the other hand, any person of clever and versatile mind can turn the whole thing around and show how I have projected my subjective contents into the symbolism of the hexagrams. Such a critique, though catastrophic from the standpoint of Western rationality, does no harm to the function of the I Ching. On the contrary, the Chinese sage would smilingly tell me: "Don't you see how useful the I Ching is in making you project your hitherto unrealized thoughts into its abstruse symbolism? You could have written your foreword without ever realizing what an avalanche of misunderstanding might be released by it."

The Chinese standpoint does not concern itself as to the attitude one takes toward the performance of the oracle. It is only we who are puzzled, because we trip time and again over our prejudice, viz., the notion of causality. The ancient wisdom of the East lays stress upon the fact that the intelligent individual realizes his own thoughts, but not in the least upon the way in which he does it. The less one thinks about the theory of the I Ching, the more soundly one sleeps.

It would seem to me that on the basis of this example an unprejudiced reader would now be in a position to form at least a tentative judgment on the operation of the I Ching. More cannot be expected from a simple introduction. If by means of this demonstration I have succeeded in elucidating the psychological phenomenology of the I Ching, I shall have carried out my purpose. As to the thousands of questions, doubts, and criticisms that this singular book stirs up — I cannot answer these. The I Ching does not offer itself with proofs and results; it does not vaunt itself, nor is it easy to approach. Like a part of nature, it waits until it is discovered. It offers neither facts nor power, but for lovers of self-knowledge, of wisdom — if there be such — it seems to be the right book. To one person its spirit appears as clear as day; to another, shadowy as twilight; to a third, dark as night. He who is not pleased by it does not have to use it, and he who is against it is not obliged to find it true. Let it go forth into the world for the benefit of those who can discern its meaning.

C. G. JUNG

Introduction
by Richard Wilhelm

The Book of Changes — I Ching in Chinese — is unquestionably one of the most important books in the world's literature. Its origin goes back to mythical antiquity, and it has occupied the attention of the most eminent scholars of China down to the present day. Nearly all that is greatest and most significant in the three thousand years of Chinese cultural history has either taken its inspiration from this book, or has exerted an influence on the interpretation of its text. Therefore it may safely be said that the seasoned wisdom of thousands of years has gone into the making of the I Ching. Small wonder then that both of the two branches of Chinese philosophy, Confucianism and Taoism, have their common roots here. The book sheds new light on many a secret hidden in the often puzzling modes of thought of that mysterious sage, Lao-tse, and of his pupils, as well as on many ideas that appear in the Confucian tradition as axioms, accepted without further examination.

Indeed, not only the philosophy of China but its science and statecraft as well have never ceased to draw from the spring of wisdom in the I Ching, and it is not surprising that this alone, among all the Confucian classics, escaped the great burning of the books under Ch'in Shih Huang Ti. Even the common-places of everyday life in China are saturated with its influence. In going through the streets of a Chinese city, one will find, here and there at a street corner, a fortune teller sitting behind a neatly covered table, brush and tablet at hand, ready to draw from the ancient book of wisdom pertinent counsel and information on life's minor perplexities. Not only that, but the very signboards adorning the houses —perpendicular wooden panels done in gold on black lacquer — are covered with inscriptions whose flowery language again and again recalls thoughts and quotations from the I Ching. Even the policy makers of so modern a state as Japan, distinguished for their astuteness, do not scorn to refer to it for counsel in difficult situations.

In the course of time, owing to the great repute for wisdom attaching to the Book of Changes, a large body of occult doctrines extraneous to it — some of them possibly not even Chinese in origin — have come to be connected with its teachings. The Ch'in and Han dynasties saw the beginning of a formalistic natural philosophy that sought to embrace the entire world of thought in a system of number symbols. Combining a rigorously consistent, dualistic yin-yang doctrine with the doctrine of the "five stages of change" taken from the Book of History, it forced Chinese philosophical thinking more and more into a rigid formalization. Thus increasingly hairsplitting cabalistic speculations came to envelop the Book of Changes in a cloud of mystery, and by forcing everything of the past and of the future into this system of numbers, created for the I Ching the reputation of being a book of unfathomable profundity. These speculations are also to blame for the fact that the seeds of a free Chinese natural science, which undoubtedly existed at the time of Mo Ti and his pupils, were killed, and replaced by a sterile tradition of writing and reading books that was wholly removed from experience. This is the reason why China has for so long presented to Western eyes a picture of hopeless stagnation.

Yet we must not overlook the fact that apart from this mechanistic number mysticism, a living stream of deep human wisdom was constantly flowing through the channel of this book into everyday life, giving to China's great civilization that ripeness of wisdom, distilled through the ages, which we wistfully admire in the remnants of this last truly autochthonous culture.

What is the Book of Changes actually? In order to arrive at an understanding of the book and its teachings, we must first of all boldly strip away the dense overgrowth of interpretations that have read into it all sorts of extraneous ideas. This is equally necessary whether we are dealing with the superstitions and mysteries of old Chinese sorcerers or the no less superstitious theories of modern Estropean scholars who try to interpret all historical cultures in terms of their experience of primitive savages. We must hold here to the fundamental principle that the Book of Changes is to be explained in the light of its own content and of the era to which it belongs. With this the darkness lightens perceptibly and we realize that this book, though a very profound work, does not offer greater difficulties to our understanding than any other book that has come down through a long history from antiquity to our time.

THE USE OF THE BOOK OF CHANGES
The Book of Oracles

At the outset, the Book of Changes was a collection of linear signs to be used as oracles. In antiquity, oracles were everywhere in use; the oldest among them confined themselves to the answers yes and no. This type of oracular pronouncement is likewise the basis of the Book of Changes.
"Yes" was indicated by a simple unbroken line (___), and
"No" by a broken line (_ _). However, the need for greater differentiation seems to have been felt at an early date, and the single lines were combined in pairs:

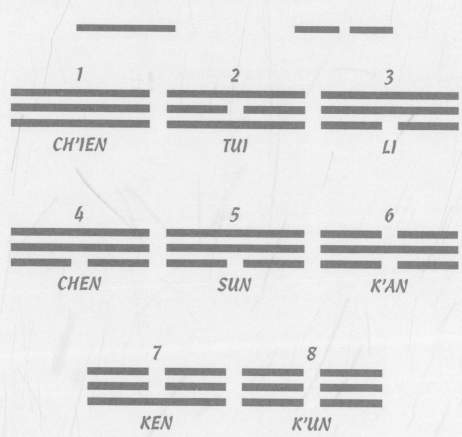

These eight images came to have manifold meanings. They represented certain processes in nature corresponding with their inherent character. Further, they represented a family consisting of father, mother, three sons, and three daughters, not in the mythological sense in which the Greek gods peopled Olympus, but in what might be called an abstract sense, that is, they represented not objective entities but functions.

To each of these combinations a third line was then added. In this way the eight trigrams came into being. These eight trigrams were conceived as images of all that happens in heaven and on earth. At the same time, they were held to he in a state of continual transition, one changing into another, just as transition from one phenomenon to another is continually taking place in the physical world. Here we have the fundamental concept of the Book of Changes. The eight trigrams are symbols standing for changing transitional states; they are images that are constantly undergoing change. Attention centres not on things in their state of being — as is chiefly the case in the Occident — but upon their movements in change. The eight trigrams therefore are not representations of things as such but of their tendencies in movement.

These eight images came to have manifold meanings. They represented certain processes in nature corresponding with their inherent character. Further, they represented a family consisting of father, mother, three sons, and three daughters, not in the mythological sense in which the Greek gods peopled Olympus, but in what might be called an abstract sense, that is, they represented not objective entities but functions.

TRIGRAM ATTRIBUTES

The sons represent the principle of movement in its various stages — beginning of movement, danger in movement, rest and completion of movement.

The daughters represent devotion in its various stages — gentle penetration, clarity and adaptability, and joyous tranquillity.

In order to achieve a still greater multiplicity, these eight images were combined with one another at a very early date, whereby a total of sixty-four signs was obtained. Each of these sixty-four signs consists of six lines, either positive or negative. Each line is thought of as capable of change, and whenever a line changes, there is a change also of the situation represented by the given hexagram. Let us take for example the hexagram K'un, THE RECEPTIVE, earth:

It represents the nature of the earth, strong in devotion; among the seasons it stands for late autumn, when all the forces of life are at rest. If the lowest line changes, we have the hexagram Fu, RETURN:

The latter represents thunder, the movement that stirs anew within the earth at the time of the solstice; it symbolizes the return of light.

As this example shows, all of the lines of a hexagram do not necessarily change; it depends entirely on the character of a given line. A line whose nature is positive, with an increasing dynamism, turns into its opposite, a negative line, whereas a positive line of lesser strength remains unchanged. The same principle holds for the negative lines.

Positive lines that move are designated by the number 9, and negative lines that move by the number 6, while non-moving lines, which serve only as structural matter in the hexagram, without intrinsic meaning of their own, are represented by the number 7 (positive) or the number 8 (negative). Thus, when the text reads, "Nine at the beginning means..." this is the equivalent of saying: "When the positive line in the first place is represented by the number 9, it has the following meaning..." If, on the other hand, the line is represented by the number 7, it is disregarded in interpreting the oracle. The same principle holds for lines represented by the numbers 6 and 8 respectively. See page 38: Throwing The Coins!

We may obtain the hexagram named in the example above — K'un, THE RECEPTIVE — in the following form:

8 at the top
8 in the fifth place
8 in the fourth place
8 in the third place
8 in the second place
6 at the beginning

Hence the five upper lines are not taken into account; only the 6 at the beginning has an independent meaning, and by its transformation into its opposite, the situation K'un, THE RECEPTIVE, becomes the situation Fu, RETURN:

In this way we have a series of situations symbolically expressed by lines, and through the movement of these lines the situations can change one into another. On the other hand, such change does not necessarily occur, for when a hexagram is made up of lines represented by the numbers 7 and 8 only, there is no movement within it, and only its aspect as a whole is taken into consideration.

In addition to the law of change and to the images of the states of change as given in the sixty-four hexagrams, another factor to be considered is the course of action. Each situation demands the action proper to it. In every situation, there is a right and a wrong course of action. Obviously, the right course brings good fortune and the wrong course brings misfortune. Which, then, is the right course in any given case? This question was the decisive factor. As a result, the I Ching was lifted above the level of an ordinary book of soothsaying. If a fortune teller on reading the cards tells her client that she will receive a letter with money from America in a week, there is nothing for the woman to do but wait until the letter comes — or does not come. In this case what is foretold is fate, quite independent of what the individual may do or not do. For this reason fortune telling lacks moral significance. When it happened for the first time in China that someone, on being told the auguries for the future, did not let the matter rest there but asked, "What am I to do?" the book of divination had to become a book of wisdom.

It was reserved for King Wen, who lived about 1150 B.C., and his son, the Duke of Chou, to bring about this change. They endowed the hitherto mute hexagrams and lines, from which the future had to he divined as an individual matter in each case, with definite counsels for correct conduct. Thus the individual came to share in shaping fate. For his actions intervened as determining factors in world events, the more decisively so, the earlier he was able with the aid of the Book of Changes to recognize situations in their germinal phases. The germinal phase is the crux. As long as things are in their beginnings they can be controlled, but once they have grown to their full consequences they acquire a power so overwhelming that man stands impotent before them. Thus the Book of Changes became a book of divination of a very special kind. The hexagrams and lines in their movements and changes mysteriously reproduced the movements and changes of the macrocosm. By throwing the coins, one could attain a point of vantage from which it was possible to survey the condition of things. Given this perspective, the words of the oracle would indicate what should be done to meet the need of the time.

The only thing about all this that seems strange to our modern sense is the method of learning the nature of a situation through the throwing of coins. This procedure was regarded as mysterious, however, simply in the sense that the manipulation of the coins makes it possible for the unconscious in man to become active. All individuals are not equally fitted to consult the oracle. It requires a clear and tranquil mind, receptive to the cosmic influences hidden in the coins.

Trigram Attributes

Ch'ien	Heaven Day	Creative Strong	Early Winter Ice
K'un	Earth Night	Yielding Nourishing	Early Autumn Warm
Chen	Thunder	Active Exciting	Spring Earthquake
K'an	Water Moon	Dangerous Abysmal	Mid Winter Cloudy
Ken	Mountain	Keeping Still Perverse	Late Winter Stillness
Sun	Wind Wood	Gentle Gradual	Early Summer Stillness
Li	Fire Sun	Conscious Depending	Mid Summer Lighting
Tui	Lake	Joyful Fullness	Late Autumn Rain

THE BOOK OF WISDOM

Of far greater significance than the use of the Book of Changes as an oracle is its other use, namely, as a book of wisdom. Laotse knew this book, and some of his profoundest aphorisms were inspired by it. Indeed, his whole thought is permeated with its teachings. Confucius too, knew the Book of Changes and devoted himself to reflection upon it. He probably wrote down some of his interpretative comments and imparted others to his pupils in oral teaching. The Book of Changes as edited and annotated by Confucius is the version that has come down to our time.

If we inquire as to the philosophy that pervades the book, we can confine ourselves to a few basically important concepts. The underlying idea of the whole is the idea of change. It is related in the Analects that Confucius, standing by a river, said: "Everything flows on and on like this river, without pause, day and night." This expresses the idea of change. He who has perceived the meaning of change fixes his attention no longer on transitory individual things but on the immutable, eternal law at work in all change. This law is the tao of Lao-tse, the course of things, the principle of the one in the many. That it may become manifest, a decision, a postulate, is necessary. This fundamental postulate is the "great primal beginning" of all that exists, t'ai chi — in its original meaning, the "ridgepole." Later Chinese philosophers devoted much thought to this idea of a primal beginning. A still earlier beginning, wu chi, was represented by the symbol of a circle. Under this conception, t'ai chi was represented by the circle divided into the light and the dark, yang and yin.

This symbol has also played a significant part in India and Europe. However, speculations of a gnostic-dualistic character are foreign to the original thought of the I Ching; what it posits is simply the ridgepole, the line. With this line, which in itself represents oneness, duality comes into the world, for the line at the same time posits an above and a below, a right and left, front and back-in a word, the world of the opposites.

These opposites became known under the names yin and yang and created a great stir, especially in the transition period between the Ch'in and Han dynasties, in the centuries just before our era, when there was an entire school of yin-yang doctrine. At that time, the Book of Changes was much in use as a book of magic, and people read into the text all sorts of things not originally there. This doctrine of yin and yang, of the female and the male as primal principles, has naturally also attracted much attention among foreign students of Chinese thought. Following the usual bent, some of these have predicated in it a primitive phallic symbolism, with all the accompanying connotations.

To the disappointment of such discoverers it must be said that there is nothing to indicate this in the original meaning of the words yin and yang. In its primary meaning yin is "the cloudy," "the overcast," and yang means actually "banners waving in the sun," that is, something "shone upon," or bright. By transference the two concepts were applied to the light and dark sides of a mountain or of a river. In the case of a mountain the southern is the bright side and the northern the dark side, while in the case of a river seen from above, it is the northern side that is bright (yang), because it reflects the light, and the southern side that is in shadow (yin). Thence the two expressions were carried over into the Book of Changes and applied to the two alternating primal states of being. It should be pointed out, however, that the terms yin and yang do not occur in this derived sense either in the actual text of the book or in the oldest commentaries. Their first occurrence is in the Great Commentary, which already shows Taoistic influence in some parts. In the Commentary on the Decision the terms used for the opposites are "the firm" and "the yielding," not yang and yin.

However, no matter what names are applied to these forces, it is certain that the world of being arises out of their change and interplay. Thus change is conceived of partly as the continuous transformation of the one force into the other and partly as a cycle of complexes of phenomena, in themselves connected, such as day and night, summer and winter. Change is not meaningless — if it were, there could be no knowledge of it — but subject to the universal law, tao.

The second theme fundamental to the Book of Changes is its theory of ideas. The eight trigrams are images not so much of objects as of states of change. This view is associated with the concept expressed in the teachings of Lao-tse, as also in those of Confucius, that every event in the visible world is the effect of an "image," that is, of an idea in the unseen world. Accordingly, everything that happens on earth is only a reproduction, as it were, of an event in a world beyond our sense perception, as regards its occurrence in time, it is later than the suprasensible event. The holy men and sages, who are in contact with those higher spheres, have access to these ideas through direct intuition and are therefore able to intervene decisively in events in the world. Thus man is linked with heaven, the suprasensible world of ideas, and with earth, the material world of visible things, to form with these a trinity of the primal powers.

This theory of ideas is applied in a twofold sense. The Book of Changes shows the images of events and also the unfolding of conditions in statu nascendi. Thus, in discerning with its help the seeds of things to come, we learn to foresee the future as well as to understand the past. In this way the images on which the hexagrams are based serve as patterns for timely action in the situations indicated.

The third element fundamental to the Book of Changes are the judgments. The judgments clothe the images in words, as it were; they indicate whether a given action will bring good fortune or misfortune, remorse or humiliation. The judgments make it possible for a man to make a decision to desist from a course of action indicated by the situation of the moment but harmful in the long run. In this way he makes himself independent of the tyranny of events. In its judgments, and in the interpretations attached to it from the time of Confucius on the Book of Changes opens to the reader the richest treasure of Chinese wisdom; at the same time it affords him a comprehensive view of the varieties of human experience, enabling him thereby to shape his life of his own sovereign will into an organic whole and so to direct it that it comes into accord with the ultimate tao lying at the root of all that exists.

The History of the Book of Change

In Chinese literature four holy men are cited as the authors of the Book of Changes, namely, Fu Hsi, King Wen, the Duke of Chou, and Confucius. Fu Hsi is a legendary figure representing the era of hunting and fishing and of the invention of cooking. The fact that he is designated as the inventor of the linear signs of the Book of Changes means that they have been held to be of such antiquity that they antedate historical memory. Moreover, the eight trigrams have names that do not occur in any other connection in the Chinese language, and because of this they have even been thought to be of foreign origin. At all events, they are not archaic characters, as some have been led to believe by the half accidental, half intentional resemblances to them appearing here and there among ancient characters.

The eight trigrams are found occurring in various combinations at a very early date. Two collections belonging to antiquity are mentioned: first, the Book of Changes of the Hsia dynasty, is called Lien Shan, which is said to have begun with the hexagram Ken, KEEPING STILL, mountain; second, the Book of Changes dating from the Shang dynasty, is entitled Kuei Ts'ang, which began with the hexagram K'un, THE RECEPTIVE. The latter circumstance is mentioned in passing by Confucius himself as a historical fact. It is difficult to say whether the names of the sixty-four hexagrams were then in existence, and if so, whether they were the same as those in the present Book of Changes.

According to general tradition, which we have no reason to challenge, the present collection of sixty-four hexagrams originated with King Wen, progenitor of the Chou dynasty. He is said to have added brief judgments to the hexagrams during his imprisonment at the hands of the tyrant Chou Hsin. The text pertaining to the individual lines originated with his son, the Duke of Chou. This form of the book, entitled the Changes of Chou, was in use as an oracle throughout the Chou period, as can be proven from a number of the ancient historical records.

This was the status of the book at the time Confucius came upon it. In his old age he gave it intensive study, and it is highly probable that the Commentary on the Decision (T'uan Chuan) is his work. The Commentary on the Images also goes back to him, though less directly. A third treatise, a very valuable and detailed commentary on the individual lines, compiled by his pupils or by their successors, in the form of questions and answers, survives only in fragments.

Among the followers of Confucius, it would appear, it was principally Pu Shang (Tzú Hsia) who spread the knowledge of the Book of Changes. With the development of philosophical speculation, as reflected in the Great Learning (Ta Hsüeh) and the Doctrine of the Mean (Chung Yung), this type of philosophy exercised an ever increasing influence upon the interpretation of the Book of Changes. A literature grew up around the book, fragments of which — some dating from an early and some from a later time — are to be found in the so-called Ten Wings. They differ greatly with respect to content and intrinsic value.

The Book of Changes escaped the fate of the other classics at the time of the famous burning of the books under the tyrant Ch'in Shih Huang Ti. Hence, if there is anything in the legend that the burning alone is responsible for the mutilation of the texts of the old books, the I Ching at least should be intact; but this is not the case. In reality it is the vicissitudes of the centuries, the collapse of ancient cultures, and the change in the system of writing that are to be blamed for the damage suffered by all ancient works.

After the Book of Changes had become firmly established as a book of divination and magic in the time of Ch'in Shih Huang Ti, the entire school of magicians (fang shih) of the Ch'in and Han dynasties made it their prey. And the yin-yang doctrine, which was probably introduced through the work of Tsou Yen, and later promoted by Tung Chung Shu, Liu Hsin, and Liu Hsiang, ran riot in connection with the interpretation of the I Ching.

The task of clearing away all this rubbish was reserved for a great and wise scholar, Wang Pi, who wrote about the meaning of the Book of Changes as a book of wisdom, not as a book of divination. He soon found emulation, and the teachings of the yin-yang school of magic were displaced, in relation to the book, by a philosophy of statecraft that was gradually developing. In the Sung period, the I Ching was used as a basis for the t'ai chi t'u doctrine — which was probably not of Chinese origin — until the appearance of the elder Ch'eng Tzú's very good commentary.
It had become customary to separate the old commentaries contained in the Ten Wings and to place them with the individual hexagrams to which they refer. Thus the book became by degrees entirely a textbook relating to

statecraft and the philosophy of life. Then Chu Hsi attempted to rehabilitate it as a book of oracles; in addition to a short and precise commentary on the I Ching, he published an introduction to his investigations concerning the art of divination.

The critical-historical school of the last dynasty also took the Book of Changes in hand. However, because of their opposition to the Sung scholars and their preference for the Han commentators, who were nearer in point of time to the compilation of the Book of Changes, they were less successful here than in their treatment of the other classics. For the Han commentators were in the last analysis sorcerers, or were influenced by theories of magic. A very good edition was arranged in the K'ang Hsi period, under the title Chou I Che Chung; it presents the text and the wings separately and includes the best commentaries of all periods. This is the edition on which the present translation is based.

R.W.

THROWING THE COINS

Three coins are taken up and thrown down together, and each throw gives a line. The inscribed side counts as yin, with the value of 2, and the reverse side counts as yang with the value of 3. From this the character of the line is derived. If all three coins are yang, the line is 9. If all three are yin, it is a 6. Two yin and one yang yield a 7 and two yang and a yin yield an 8.

The first throw is recorded as the lowest line of the six-line hexagram, the second throw shows the hexagram for the second lowest line, and throw by throw you build up from the bottom until you have the entire six-line hexagram constructed.

See the coin arrangement below giving the coin combination for either broken or unbroken lines.

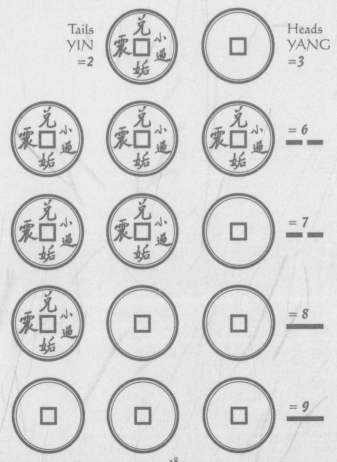

UPPER TRIGRAM → / LOWER TRIGRAM ↓	CH'IEN	CHEN	K'AN	KEN	K'UN	SUN	LI	TUI
CH'IEN	1	34	5	26	11	9	14	43
CHEN	25	51	3	27	24	42	21	17
K'AN	6	40	29	4	7	59	64	47
KEN	33	62	39	52	15	53	56	31
K'UN	12	16	8	23	2	20	35	45
SUN	44	32	48	18	46	57	50	28
LI	13	55	63	22	36	37	30	49
TUI	10	54	60	41	19	61	38	58

Table of Sixty-Four Hexagrams

On completing the throwing of the coins to determine your hexagram refer to page 39. to locate its number. The hexagram can also be identified by referring to the chart on pages 42-43. Once you have the number of your hexagram turn to the appropriate number on the following pages for a general summery, then locate the hexagram number following the general summaries for a more detailed analysis.

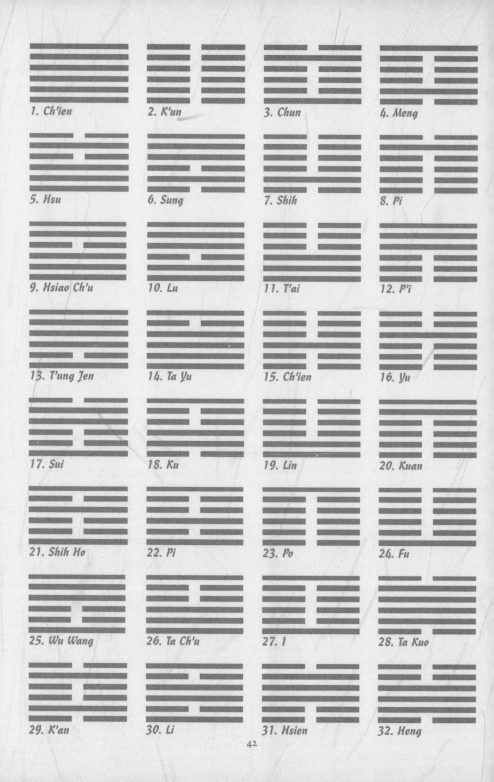

1. Ch'ien

2. K'un

3. Chun

4. Meng

5. Hsu

6. Sung

7. Shih

8. Pi

9. Hsiao Ch'u

10. Lu

11. T'ai

12. P'i

13. T'ung Jen

14. Ta Yu

15. Ch'ien

16. Yu

17. Sui

18. Ku

19. Lin

20. Kuan

21. Shih Ho

22. Pi

23. Po

24. Fu

25. Wu Wang

26. Ta Ch'u

27. I

28. Ta Kuo

29. K'an

30. Li

31. Hsien

32. Heng

33. Tun

34. Ta Chuang

35. Chin

36. Ming I

37. Chia Jen

38. K'uei

39. Chien

40. Shieh

41. Sun

42. I

43. Kuai

44. Kou

45. Ts'ui

46. Sheng

47. K'un

48. Ching

49. Ko

50. Ting

51. Chen

52. Ken

53. Chien

54. Kuei Mei

55. Feng

56. Lu

57. Sun

58. Tui

59. Huan

60. Chieh

61. Chung Fu

62. Hsiao Kuo

63. Chi Chi

64. Wei Chi

BRIEF DESCRIPTION OF THE
SIXTY-FOUR HEXAGRAMS

1. CH'IEN / The Creative

The first hexagram is made up of six unbroken lines. These unbroken lines stand for the primal power, which is light-giving, active, strong, and of the spirit. The hexagram is consistently strong in character, and since it is without weakness, its essence is power or energy. Its image is heaven. Its energy is represented as unrestricted by any fixed conditions in space and is therefore conceived of as motion. Time is regarded as the basis of this motion. Thus the hexagram includes also the power of time and the power of persisting in time, that is, duration. The power represented by the hexagram is to be interpreted in a dual sense in terms of its action on the universe and of its action on the world of men. In relation to the universe, the hexagram expresses the strong, creative action of the Deity. In relation to the human world, it denotes the creative action of the holy man or sage, of the ruler or leader of men, who through his power awakens and develops their higher nature.

2 K'UN / The Receptive

This hexagram is made up of broken lines only. The broken lines represents the dark, yielding, receptive primal power of yin. The attribute of the hexagram is devotion; its image is the earth. It is the perfect complement of THE CREATIVE—the complement, not the opposite, for the Receptive does not combat the Creative but completes it . It represents nature in contrast to spirit, earth in contrast to heaven, space as against time, the female-maternal as against the male-paternal. However, as applied to human affairs, the principle of this complementary relationship is found not only in the relation between man and woman, but also in that between prince and minister and between father and son. Indeed, even in the individual this duality appears in the coexistence of the spiritual world and the world of the senses. But strictly speaking there is no real dualism here, because there is a clearly defined hierarchic relationship between the two principles. In itself of course the Receptive is just as important as the Creative, but the attribute of devotion defines the place occupied by this primal power in relation to the Creative. For the Receptive must be activated and led by the Creative; then it is productive of good. Only when it abandons this position and tries to stand as an equal side by side with the Creative, does it become evil. The result then is opposition to and struggle against the Creative, which is productive of evil to both.

3. CHUN / Difficulty at the Beginning

The name of the hexagram, Chun, really connotes a blade of grass pushing against an obstacle as it sprouts out of the earth—hence the meaning, "difficulty at the beginning." The hexagram indicates the way in which heaven and earth bring forth individual beings. It is their first meeting, which is beset with difficulties. The lower trigram Chen is the Arousing; its motion is upward and its image is thunder. The upper trigram K'an stands for the Abysmal, the dangerous. Its motion is downward and its image is rain. The situation points to teeming, chaotic profusion; thunder and rain fill the air. But the chaos clears up. While the Abysmal sinks, the upward movement eventually passes beyond the danger. A thunderstorm brings release from tension, and all things breathe freely again.

4. MENG / Youthful Folly

In this hexagram we are reminded of youth and folly in two different ways. The image of the upper trigram, Ken, is the mountain, that of the lower, K'an, is water; the spring rising at the foot of the mountain is the image of inexperienced youth. Keeping still is the attribute of the upper trigram; that of the lower is the abyss, danger. Stopping in perplexity on the brink of a dangerous abyss is a symbol of the folly of youth. However, the two trigrams also show the way of overcoming the follies of youth. Water is something that of necessity flows on. When the spring gushes forth, it does not know at first where it will go. But its steady flow fills up the deep place blocking its progress, and success is attained.

5. HSU / Waiting (Nourishment)

All beings have need of nourishment from above. But the gift of food comes in its own time, and for this one must wait. This hexagram shows the clouds in the heavens, giving rain to refresh all that grows and to provide mankind with food and drink. The rain will come in its own time. We cannot make it come; we have to wait for it. The idea of waiting is further suggested by the attributes of the two trigrams—strength within, danger in from. Strength in the face of danger does not plunge ahead but bides its time, whereas weakness in the face of danger grows agitated and has not the patience to wait.

6. SUNG / Conflict

The upper trigram, whose image is heaven, has an upward movement; the lower trigram, water, in accordance with its nature tends downward. Thus the two halves move away from each other, giving rise to the idea of conflict. The attribute of the Creative is strength, that of the Abysmal is danger, guile. Where cunning has force before it, there is conflict. A third indication of conflict, in terms of character, is presented by the combination of deep cunning within and fixed determination outwardly. A person of this character will certainly be quarrelsome.

7. SHIH / The Army

This hexagram is made up of the trigrams K'an, water, and K'un, earth, and thus it symbolizes the ground water stored up in the earth. In the same way military strength is stored up in the mass of the people—invisible in times of peace but always ready for use as a source of power. The attributes of the two trig rams are danger inside and obedience must prevail outside. Of the individual lines, the one that controls the hexagram is the strong nine in the second place, to which the other lines, all yielding, are subordinate. This line indicates a commander, because it stands in the middle of one of the two trigrams. But since it is in the lower rather than the upper trigram, it represents not the ruler but the efficient general, who maintains obedience in the army by his authority.

8. PI / Holding Together [union]

The waters on the surface of the earth flow together wherever they can, as for example in the ocean, where all the rivers come together. Symbolically this connotes holding together and the laws that regulate it. The same idea is suggested by the fact that all the lines of the hexagram except the fifth, the place of the ruler, are yielding. The yielding lines hold together because they are influenced by a man of strong will in the leading position, a man who is their centre of union. Moreover, this strong and guiding personality in turn holds together with the others, finding in them the complement of his own nature.

9. HSIAO CH'U / The Taming Power of the Small

This hexagram means the force of the small—the power of the shadowy—that restrains, tames, impedes. A weak line in the fourth place, that of the minister, holds the five strong lines in check. In the Image it is the wind blowing across the sky. The wind restrains the clouds, the rising breath of the Creative, and makes them grow dense, but as yet is not strong enough to turn them to rain. The hexagram presents a configuration of circumstances in which a strong element is temporarily held in leash by a weak element. It is only through gentleness that this can have a successful outcome.

10. LU / Treading [Conduct]

The name of the hexagram means on the one hand the right way of conducting oneself. Heaven, the father, is above, and the lake, the youngest daughter, is below. This shows the difference between high and low, upon which composure correct social conduct, depends. On the other hand the word for the name of the hexagram, TREADING, means literally treading upon something. The small and cheerful [Tui] treads upon the large and strong [Ch'ien]. The direction of movement of the two primary trigrams is upward. The fact that the strong treads on the weak is not mentioned in the Book of Changes, because it is taken for granted. For the weak to take a stand against the strong is not dangerous here, because it happened in good humour [Tui] and without presumption, so that the strong man is not irritated but takes it all in good part.

11. T'AI / Peace

The Receptive, which moves downward, stands above; the Creative, which moves upward, is below. Hence their influences meet and are in harmony, so that all living things bloom and prosper. This hexagram belongs to the first month (February-March), at which time the forces of nature prepare the new spring.

12. P'I / Standstill [Stagnation]

This hexagram is the opposite of the preceding one. Heaven is above, drawing farther and farther away, while the earth below sinks farther into the depths. The creative powers are not in relation. It is a time of standstill and decline. This hexagram is linked with the seventh month (August-September), when the year has passed its zenith and autumnal decay is setting in.

13. T'UNG JEN / Fellowship with Men

The image of the upper trigram Ch'ien is heaven, and that of the lower, Li, is flame. It is the nature of fire to flame up to the heaven. This gives the idea of fellowship. IT is the second line that, by virtue of its central character, unites the five strong lines around it. This hexagram forms a complement to Shih, THE ARMY (7). In the latter, danger is within and obedience without—the character of a warlike army, which, in order to hold together, needs one strong man among the many who are weak. Here, clarity is within and strength without—the character of a peaceful union of men, which, in order to hold together, needs one yielding nature among many firm persons.

14. TA YU / Possession in Great Measure

The fire in heaven above shines far, and all things stand out in the light and become manifest. The weak fifth line occupies the place of honour and all the strong lines are in accord with it. All things come to the man who is modest and kind in a high position.

15. CH'IEN / Modesty

This hexagram is made up of the trigrams Ken, Keeping Still, mountain, and K'un. The mountain is the youngest son of the Creative, the representative of heaven and earth. It dispenses the blessings of heaven, the clouds and rain that gather round its summit, and thereafter shines forth radiant with heavenly light. This shows what modesty is and how it functions in great and strong men. K'un, the earth, stands above. Lowliness is a quality of the earth: this is the very reason why it appears in this hexagram as exalted, by being placed above the mountain. This shows how modesty functions in lowly, simple people: they are lifted up by it.

16. YU / Enthusiasm

The strong line in the fourth place, that of the leading official, meets with response and obedience from all the other lines, which are all weak. The attribute of the upper trigram, Chen, is movement; the attributes of K'un, the lower, are obedience and devotion. This begins a movement that meets with devotion and therefore inspires enthusiasm, carrying all with it. Of great importance, furthermore, is the law of movement along the line of least resistance, which in this hexagram is enunciated as the law for natural events and for human life

17. SUI / Following

The trigram Tui, the Joyous, whose attribute is gladness, is above; Chen, the Arousing, which has the attribute of movement, is below. Joy in movement induces following. The Joyous is the youngest daughter, while the Arousing is the eldest son. An older man defers to a young girl and shows her consideration. By this he moves her to follow him.

18. KU / Work on what has been spoiled [Decay]

The Chinese character ku represents a bowl in whose contents worms are breeding. This means decay. It has come about because the gentle indifference in the lower trigram has come together with the rigid inertia of the upper, and the result is stagnation. Since this implies guilt, the conditions embody a demand for removal of the cause. Hence the meaning of the hexagram is not simply "what has been spoiled" but "work on what has been spoiled".

19. LIN / Approach

The Chinese word lin has a range of meanings that is not exhausted by any single word of another language. The ancient explanations in the Book of Changes give as its first meaning, "becoming great." What becomes great are the two strong lines growing into the hexagram from below; the light-giving power expands with them. The meaning is then further extended to include the concept of approach, especially the approach of what is lower. Finally the meaning includes the attitude of condescension of a man in high position toward the people, and in general the setting to work on affairs. This hexagram is linked with the twelfth month (January-February), when after the winter solstice, the light power begins to ascend again.

20. KUAN / Contemplation (View)

A slight variation of tonal stress gives the Chinese name for this hexagram a double meaning. It means both contemplating and being seen, in the sense of being an example. These ideas are suggested by the fact that the hexagram can be understood as picturing a type of tower characteristic of ancient China.

21. SHIH HO / Biting Through

This hexagram represents an open mouth (cf. hexagram 27) with an obstruction (in the fourth place) between the teeth. As a result the lips cannot meet. To bring them together one must bite energetically through the obstacle. Since the hexagram is made up of the trigrams for thunder and for lightning, it indicates how obstacles are forcibly removed in nature. Energetic biting through overcomes the obstacle that prevents joining of the lips; the storm with its thunder and lightning overcomes the disturbing tension in nature. Recourse to law and penalties overcomes the disturbances of harmonious social life caused by criminals and slanderers. The theme of this hexagram is a criminal lawsuit, in contradistinction to that of Sung, CONFLICT (6), which refers to civil suits.

22. PI / Grace

This hexagram shows a fire that breaks out of the secret depths of the earth and, blazing up, illuminates and beautifies the mountain, the heavenly heights. Grace—beauty of form—is necessary in any union if it is to be well ordered and pleasing rather than disordered and chaotic.

23. PO / Splitting Apart

The dark lines are about to mount upward and overthrow the last firm, light line by exerting a disintegrating influence on it. The inferior, dark forces overcome what is superior and strong, not by direct means, but by undermining it gradually and imperceptibly, so that it finally collapses. The lines of the hexagram present the image of a house, the top line being the roof, and because the roof is being shattered the house collapses. The hexagram belongs to the ninth month (October-November). The yin power pushes up ever more powerfully and is about to supplant the yang power altogether.

24. FU / Return (The Turning Point)

The idea of a turning point arises from the fact that after the dark lines have pushed all of the light lines upward and out of the hexagram, another light line enters the hexagram from below. The time of darkness is past. The winter solstice brings the victory of light. This hexagram is linked with the eleventh month, the month of the solstice (December-January).

25. WU WANG / Innocence (The Unexpected)

Ch'ien, heaven is above; Chen, movement, is below. The lower trigram Chen is under the influence of the strong line it has received form above, from heaven. When, in accord with this, movement follows the law of heaven, man is innocent and without guile. His mind is natural and true, unshadowed by reflection or ulterior designs. For wherever conscious purpose is to be seen, there the truth and innocence of nature have been lost. Nature that is not directed by the spirit is not true but degenerate nature. Starting out with the idea of the natural, the train of thought in part goes somewhat further and thus the hexagram includes also the idea of the fundamental or unexpected.

26. TA CH'U / The Taming Power of the Great

The Creative is tamed by Ken, Keeping Still. This produces great power, a situation in contrast to that of the ninth hexagram, Hsiao Ch'u, THE TAMING POWER OF THE SMALL, in which the Creative is tamed by the Gentle alone. There one weak line must tame five strong lines, but here four strong lines are restrained by two weak lines; in addition to a minister, there is a prince, and the restraining power therefore is afar stronger. The hexagram has a threefold meaning, expressing different aspects of the concept "Holding firm." Heaven within the mountain gives the idea of holding firm in the sense of holding together; the trigram Ken which holds the trigram ch'ien still, gives the idea of holding firm in the sense of holding back; the third idea is that of holding firm in the sense of caring for and nourishing. This last is suggested by the fact that a strong line at the top, which is the ruler of the hexagram, is honoured and tended as a sage. The third of these meanings also attaches specifically to this strong line at the top, which represents the sage.

27. I / Corners of the Mouth (Providing Nourishment)

This hexagram is a picture of an open mouth; above and below are firm lines of the lips, and between them the opening. Starting with the mouth, through which we take food for nourishment, the thought leads to nourishment itself. Nourishment of oneself, specifically of the body, is represented in the three lower lines, while the three upper lines represent nourishment and care of others, in a higher, spiritual sense.

28. TA KUO / Preponderance of the Great

This hexagram consists of four strong lines inside and two weak lines outside. When the strong are outside and the weak inside, all is well and there is nothing out of balance, nothing extraordinary in the situation. Here, however, the opposite is the case. The hexagram represents a beam that is thick and heavy in the middle but too weak at the ends. This is a condition that cannot last; it must be changed, must pass, or misfortune will result.

29. K'AN / The Abysmal (Water)

This hexagram consists of a doubling of the trigram K'an. It is one of the eight hexagrams in which doubling occurs. The trigram K'an means a plunging in. A yang line has plunged in between two yin lines and is closed in by them like water in a ravine. The trigram K'an is also the middle son. The Receptive has obtained the middle line of the Creative, and thus K'an develops. As an image it represents water, the water that comes from above and is in motion on earth in streams and rivers, giving rise to all life on earth. In man's world K'an represents the heart, the soul locked up within the body, the principle of light inclosed in the dark—that is, reason. The name of the hexagram, because the trigram is doubled, has the additional meaning, "repetition of danger." Thus the hexagram is intended to designate an objective situation to which one must become accustomed, not a subjective attitude. For danger due to a subjective attitude means either foolhardiness or guile. Hence too a ravine is used to symbolize danger; it is a situation in which a man is in the same pass as the water in a ravine, and, like the water, he can escape if he behaves correctly.

30. LI / The Clinging, Fire

This hexagram is another double sign. The trigram Li means "to cling to something," and also "brightness." A dark line clings to two light lines, one above and one below--the image of an empty space between two strong lines, whereby the two strong lines are made bright. The trigram represents the middle daughter. The Creative has incorporated the central line of the Receptive, and thus Li develops. As an image, it is fire. Fire has no definite form but clings to the burning object and thus is bright. As water pours down from heaven, so fire flames up from the earth. While K'an means the soul shut within the body, Li stands for nature in its radiance.

31. HSIEN / Influence (Wooing)

The name of the hexagram means "universal," "general," and in a figurative sense "to influence," "to stimulate." The upper trigram is Tui, the Joyous; the lower is Ken, Keeping still. By its persistent, quiet influence, the lower, rigid trigram stimulates the upper, weak trigram, which responds to this stimulation cheerfully and joyously. Ken, the lower trigram, is the youngest son; the upper, Tui, is the youngest daughter. Thus the universal mutual attraction between the sexes is represented. In courtship, the masculine principle must seize the initiative and place itself below the feminine principle. Just as the first part of book 1 begins with the hexagrams of heaven and earth, the foundations of all that exists, the second part begins with the hexagrams of courtship and marriage, the foundations of all social relationships.

32. HENG / Duration

The strong trigram Chen is above, the weak trigram Sun below. This hexagram is the inverse of the preceding one. In the latter we have influence, here we have union as an enduring condition. The two images are thunder and wind, which are likewise constantly paired phenomena. The lower trigram indicates gentleness within; the upper, movement without In the sphere of social relationships, the hexagram represents the institution of marriage as the enduring union of the sexes. During courtship the young man subordinates himself to the girl, but in marriage, which is represented by the coming together of the eldest son and the eldest daughter, the husband is the directing and moving force outside, while the wife, inside, is gentle and submissive.

33. TUN / Retreat

The power of the dark is ascending. The light retreats to security, so that the dark cannot encroach upon it. This retreat is a matter not of man's will but of natural law. Therefore in this case withdrawal is proper; it is the correct way to behave in order not to exhaust one's forces. In the calendar this hexagram is linked with the sixth month (July-August), in which the forces of winter are already showing their influence.

34. TA CHUANG / The Power of the Great

The great lines, that is, the light, strong lines, are powerful. Four light lines have entered the hexagram from below and are about to ascend higher. The upper trigram is Chen, the Arousing; the lower is Ch'ien, the Creative. Ch'ien is strong, Chen produces movement. The union of movement and strength gives the meaning of THE POWER OF THE GREAT. The hexagram is linked with the second month (March-April).

35. CHIN / Progress

The hexagram represents the sun rising over the earth. It is therefore the symbol of rapid, easy progress, which at the same time means ever widening expansion and clarity.

36. MING I / Darkening of the light

Here the sun has sunk under the earth and is therefore darkened. The name of the hexagram means literally "wounding of the bright"; hence the individual lines contain frequent references to wounding. The situation is the exact opposite of that in the foregoing hexagram. In the latter a wise man at the head of affairs has able helpers, and in company with them makes progress; here a man of dark nature is in a position of authority and brings harm to the wise and able man.

37. CHIA JEN / The Family [The Clan]

The hexagram represents the laws obtaining within the family. The strong line at the top represents the father, the lowest the son. The strong line in the fifth place represents the husband, the yielding second line the wife. On the other hand, the two strong lines in the fifth and the third place represent two brothers, and the two weak lines correlated with them in the fourth and the second place stand for their respective wives. Thus all the connections and relationships within the family find their appropriate expression. Each individual line has the character according with its place. The fact that a strong line occupies the sixth place-where a weak line might be expected-indicates very clearly the strong leadership that must come from the head of the family. The line is to be considered here not in its quality as the sixth but in its quality as the top line. THE FAMILY shows the laws operative within the household that, transferred to outside life, keep the state and the world in order. The influence that goes out from within the family is represented by the symbol of the wind created by fire.

38. K'UEI / Opposition

This hexagram is composed of the trigram Li above, i.e., flame, which burns upward, and Tui below, i.e., the lake, which seeps downward. These two movements are indirect contrast. Furthermore, LI is the second daughter and Tui the youngest daughter, and although they live in the same house they belong to different men; hence their wills are not the same but are divergently directed.

39. CHIEN / Obstruction

The hexagram pictures a dangerous abyss lying before us and a steep, inaccessible mountain rising behind us. We are surrounded by obstacles; at the same time, since the mountain has the attribute of keeping still, there is implicit a hint as to how we can extricate ourselves. The hexagram represents obstructions that appear in the course of time but that can and should be overcome. Therefore all the instruction given is directed to overcoming them.

40. HSIEH / Deliverance

Here the movement goes out of the sphere of danger. The obstacle has been removed, the difficulties are being resolved. Deliverance is not yet achieved; it is just in its beginning, and the hexagram represents its various stages.

41. SUN / Decrease

This hexagram represents a decrease of the lower trigram in favour of the upper, because the third line, originally strong, has moved up to the top, and the top line, originally weak, has replaced it. What is below is decreased to the benefit of what is above. This is out-and-out decrease. If the foundations of a building are decreased in strength and the upper walls are strengthened, the whole structure loves its stability. Likewise, a decrease in the prosperity of the people in favour of the government is out-and-out decrease. And the entire theme of the hexagram is directed to showing how this shift of wealth can take place without causing the sources of wealth can take place without causing the sources of wealth in the nation and its lower classes to fail.

42. I / Increase

The idea of increase is expressed in the fact that the strong lowest line of the upper trigram has sunk down and taken its place under the lower trigram. This conception also expresses the fundamental idea on which the Book of Changes is based. To rule truly is to serve. A sacrifice of the higher element that produces an increase of the lower is called an out-and-out increase: it indicates the spirit that alone has power to help the world.

43. KUAI / Break-through (Resoluteness)

This hexagram signifies on the one hand a break-through after a long accumulation of tension, as a swollen river breaks through its dikes, or in the manner of a cloudburst. On the other hand, applied to human conditions, it refers to the time when inferior people gradually begin to disappear. Their influence is on the wane; as a result of resolute action, a change in conditions occurs, a break-through. The hexagram is linked with the third month [April-May].

44. KOU / Coming to Meet

This hexagram indicates a situation in which the principle of darkness, after having been eliminated, furtively and unexpectedly obtrudes again from within and below. Of its own accord the female principle comes to meet the male. It is an unfavourable and dangerous situation, and we must understand and promptly prevent the possible consequences. The hexagram is linked with the fifth month [June-July], because at the summer solstice the principle of darkness gradually becomes ascendant again.

45. TS'UI / Gathering Together [Massing]

This hexagram is related in form and meaning to Pi, HOLDING TOGETHER (8). In the latter, water is over the earth; here a lake is over the earth. But since the lake is a place where water collects, the idea of gathering together is even more strongly expressed here than in the other hexagram. The same idea also arises from the fact that in the present case it is two strong lines (the fourth and the fifth) that bring about the gather together, whereas in the former case one strong line (the fifth) stands in the midst of weak lines.

46. SHENG / Pushing Upward

The lower trigam, Sun, represents wood, and the upper, K'un, means the earth. Linked with this is the idea that wood in the earth grows upward. In contrast to the meaning of Chin, PROGRESS (35), this pushing upward is associated with effort, just as a plant needs energy for pushing upward through the earth. That is why this hexagram, although it is connected with success, is associated with effort of the will. In PROGRESS the emphasis is on expansion; PUSHING UPWARD indicates rather a vertical ascent-direct rise from obscurity and lowliness to power and influence.

47. K'UN / Oppression (Exhaustion)

The lake is above, water below; the lake is empty, dried up. Exhaustion is expressed in yet another way: at the top, a dark line is holding down two light line; below, a light line is hemmed in between two dark ones. The upper trigram belongs to the principle of darkness, the lower to the principle of light. Thus everywhere superior men are oppressed and held in restraint by inferior men.

48. CHING / The Well

Wood is below, water above. The wood goes down into the earth to bring up water. The image derives from the pole-and-bucket well of ancient China. The wood represents not the buckets, which in ancient times were made of clay, but rather the wooden poles by which the water is hauled up from the well. The image also refers to the world of plants, which lift water out of the earth by means of their fibres. The well from which water is drawn conveys the further idea of an inexhaustible dispensing of nourishment.

49. KO / Revolution (Molting)

The Chinese character for this hexagram means in its original sense an animal's pelt, which is changed in the course of the year by molting. From this word is carried over to apply to the "moltings" in political life, the great revolutions connected with changes of governments. The two trigrams making up the hexagram are the same two that appear in K'uei, OPPOSITION (38), that is, the two younger daughters, Li and Tui. But while there the elder of the two daughters is above, and what results is essentially only an opposition of tendencies, here the younger daughter is above.

The influences are in actual conflict, and the forces combat each other like fire and water (lake), each trying to destroy the other. Hence the idea of revolution.

50. TING / The Caldron
The six lines construct the image of Ting, THE CALDRON; at the bottom are the legs, over them the belly, then come the ears (handles), and at the top the carrying rings. At the same time, the image suggests the idea of nourishment. The ting, cast of bronze, was the vessel that held the cooked viands in the temple of the ancestors and at banquets. The heads of the family served the food from the ting into the bowls of the guests. THE WELL (48) likewise has the secondary meaning of giving nourishment, but rather more in relation to the people. The ting, as a utensil pertaining to a refined civilisation, suggests the fostering and nourishing of able men, which redounded to the benefit of the state. This hexagram and THE WELL are the only two in the Book of Changes that represent concrete, men-made objects. Yet here too the thought has its abstract connotation. Sun, below, is wood and wind; Li, above, is flame. Thus together they stand for the flame kindled by wood and wind, which likewise suggests the idea of preparing food.

51. CHEN / The Arousing (Shock, Thunder)
The hexagram Chen represents the eldest son, who seizes rule with energy and power. A yang line develops below two yin lines and presses upward forcibly. This movement is so violent that it arouses terror. It is symbolized by thunder, which bursts forth from the earth and by its shock causes fear and trembling.

52. KEN / Keeping Still, Mountain
The image of this hexagram is the mountain, the youngest son of heaven and earth. The male principle is at the top because it strives upward by nature; the female principle is below, since the direction of its movement has come to its normal end.
In its application to man, the hexagram turns upon the problem of achieving a quiet heart. It is very difficult to bring quiet to the heart. While Buddhism strives for rest through an ebbing away of all movement in nirvana, the Book of Changes holds that rest is merely a state of polarity that always posits movement as its complement. Possibly the words of the text embody directions for the practice of yoga.

53. CHIEN / Development (Gradual Progress)
This hexagram is made up of Sun (wood, penetration) above, i.e., without, and Ken (mountain, stillness) below, i.e., within. A tree on a mountain develops slowly according to the law of its being and consequently stands firmly rooted. This gives the idea of a development that proceeds gradually, step by step. The attributes of the trigrams also point to this: within is tranquillity, which guards against precipitate actions, and without is penetration, which makes development and progress possible.

54. KUEI MEI / The Marrying Maiden

Above we have Chen, the eldest son, and below, Tui, the youngest daughter. The man leads and the girl follows him in gladness. The picture is that of the entrance of the girl into her husband's house. In all, there are four hexagrams depicting the relationship between husband and wife. Hsien, INFLUENCE, (31), describes the attraction that a young couple have for each other; Heng, DURATION (32), portrays the permanent relationships of marriage; Chien, DEVELOPMENT (53), reflects the protracted, ceremonious procedures attending THE MARRYING MAIDEN, shows a young girl under the guidance of an older man who marries her.

55. FENG / Abundance [Fullness]

Chen is movement; Li is flame, whose attribute is clarity. Clarity within, movement without-this produces greatness and abundance. The hexagram pictures a period of advanced civilisation. However, the fact that development has reached a peak suggests that this extraordinary condition of abundance cannot be maintained permanently.

56. LU / The Wanderer

The mountain, Ken, stands still; above it fire, Li, flames up and does not tarry. Therefore the two trigrams do not stay together. Strange lands and separation are the wanderer's lot. When a man is a wanderer and stranger, he should not be gruff nor overbearing. He has no large circle of acquaintances, therefore he should not give himself airs. He must be cautious and reserved; in this way he protects himself from evil. If he is obliging toward others, he wins success. A wanderer has no fixed abode; his home is the road. Therefore he must take care to remain upright and steadfast, so that he sojourns only in the proper places, associating only with good people. Then he has good fortune and can go his way unmolested.

57. SUN / The Gentle (The Penetrating, Wind)

Sun is one of the eight doubled trigrams. It is the eldest daughter and symbolizes wind or wood; it has for its attribute gentleness, which nonetheless penetrates like the wind or like growing wood with its roots. The dark principle, in itself rigid and immovable, is dissolved by the penetrating light principle, to which it subordinates itself in gentleness. In nature, it is the wind that disperses the gathered clouds, leaving the sky clear and serene. In human life it is penetrating clarity of judgment that thwarts all dark hidden motives. In the life of the community it is the powerful influence of a great personality that uncovers and breaks up those intrigues which shun the light of day.

58. TUI / The Joyous, Lake

This hexagram, like sun, is one of the eight formed by doubling of a trigram. The trigram Tui denotes the youngest daughter; it is symbolized by the smiling lake, and its attribute is joyousness. Contrary to appearances, it is not the yielding quality of the top line that accounts for joy here. The attribute of the yielding or dark principle is not joy but melancholy. However, joy is indicated by the fact that there are two strong lines within, expressing themselves through the medium of gentleness. True joy, therefore, rests on firmness and strength within, manifesting itself outwardly as yielding and gentle.

59. HUAN / Dispersion [Dissolution]

Wind blowing over water disperses it, dissolving it into foam and mist. This suggests that when a man's vital energy is dammed up within him (indicated as a danger by the attribute of the lower trigram), gentleness serves to break up and dissolve the blockage.

60. CHIEH / Limitation

A lake occupies a limited space. When more water comes into it, it overflows. Therefore limits must be set for the water. The image shows water below and water above, with the firmament between them as a limit. The Chinese word for limitation really denotes the joints that divide a bamboo stalk. In relation to ordinary life it means the thrift that sets fixed limits upon expenditures. In relation to the moral sphere it means the fixed limits that the superior man sets upon his actions-the limits of loyalty and disinterestedness.

61. CHUNG FU / Inner Truth

The wind blows over the lake and stirs the surface of the water. Thus visible effects of the invisible manifest themselves. The hexagram consists of firm lines above and below, while it is open in the centre. This indicates a heart free of prejudices and therefore open to truth. On the other hand, each of the two trigrams has a firm line in the middle; this indicates the force of inner truth in the influences they present. The attributes of the two trigrams are: above, gentleness, forbearance toward inferiors; below, joyousness in obeying superiors. Such conditions create the basis of a mutual confidence that makes achievements possible. The character of fu ("truth") is actually the picture of a bird's foot over a fledgling. It suggests the idea of brooding. An egg is hollow. The light-giving power must work to quicken it from outside, but there must be a germ of life within, if life is to be awakened. Far-reaching speculations can be linked with these ideas.

62.. HSIAO KUO / Preponderance of the Small

While in the hexagram Ta Kuo, PREPONDERANCE OF THE GREAT (28), the strong lines preponderate and are within, inclosed between weak lines at the top and bottom, the present hexagram has weak lines preponderating, though here again they are on the outside, the strong lines being within. This indeed is the basis of the exceptional situation indicated by the hexagram. When strong lines are outside, we have the hexagram I, PROVIDING NOURISHMENT (27), or Chung Fu, INNER TRUTH, (61); neither represents and exceptional state. When strong elements within preponderate, they necessarily enforce their will. This creates struggle and exceptional conditions in general. But in the present hexagram it is the weak element that perforce must mediate with the outside world. If a man occupies a position of authority for which he is by nature really inadequate, extraordinary prudence is necessary.

63. CHI CHI / After Completion

This hexagram is the evolution of T'ai PEACE (11). The transition from confusion to order is completed, and everything is in its proper place even in particulars. The strong lines are in the strong places, the weak lines in the weak places. This is a very favourable outlook, yet it gives reason for thought. For it is just when perfect equilibrium has been reached that any movement may cause order to revert to disorder. The one strong line that has moved to the top, thus effecting complete order in details, is followed by the other lines. Each moving according to its nature, and thus suddenly there arises again the hexagram P'i, STANDSTILL (12). Hence the present hexagram indicates the conditions of a time of climax, which necessitate the utmost caution.

64. WEI CHI / Before Completion

This hexagram indicates a time when the transition from disorder to order is not yet completed. The change is indeed prepared for, since all the lines in the upper trigram are in relation to those in the lower. However, they are not yet in their places. While the preceding hexagram offers an analogy to autumn, which forms the transition from summer to winter, this hexagram presents a parallel to spring, which leads out of winter's stagnation into the fruitful time of summer. With this hopeful outlook the Book of Changes come to its close.

1
ch'ien

above Ch'ien
Heaven

below Ch'ien
Heaven

1. CH'IEN
The Creative

THE JUDGEMENT

The Creative works sublime
success,
Furthering through perseverance.

THE IMAGE

The movement of heaven is full of
power.
Thus the superior man makes
himself strong and untiring.

THE LINES

Nine at the beginning means:
Hidden dragon. Do not act.

Nine in the second place means:
Dragon appearing in the field.
It furthers one to see the great man.

Nine in the third place means:
All day long the superior man is
creatively active.
At nightfall his mind is still beset
with cares.
Danger. No blame.

Nine in the fourth place means:
Wavering flight over the depths.
No blame.

Nine in the fifth place means:
Flying dragon in the heavens.
It furthers one to see the great man.

Nine at the top means:
Arrogant dragon will have cause to
repent.

When all the lines are nines, it
means:
There appears a flight of dragons
without heads.
Good fortune.

2

above K'un
The Receptive,
Earth

below K'un
The Receptive
Earth

k'un

2. K'UN
The Receptive

THE JUDGEMENT

The Receptive brings about sublime
success,
Furthering through the perseverance
of a mare.
If the superior man undertakes
something and tries to lead,
He goes astray;
But if he follows, he finds guidance.
It is favorable to find friends in
the west and south,
To forego friends in the east and
north.
Quiet perseverance brings good
fortune.

THE IMAGE

The earth's condition is receptive
devotion.
Thus the superior man who has
breadth of character
Carries the outer world.

THE LINES

Six at the beginning means:
When there is hoarfrost underfoot,
Solid ice is not far off.

Six in the second place means:
Straight, square, great.
Without purpose,
Yet nothing remains unfurthered.

Six in the third place means:
Hidden lines.
One is able to remain persevering.
If by chance you are in the service of
a king,
Seek not works, but bring to
completion.

Six in the fourth place means:
A tied-up sack. No blame, no praise.

Six in the fifth place means:
A yellow lower garment brings
supreme good fortune.

Six at the top means:
Dragons fight in the meadow.
Their blood is black and yellow.

When all the lines are sixes, it
means:
Lasting perseverance furthers.

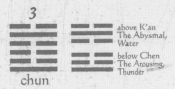

3

chun

above K'an
The Abysmal,
Water

below Chen
The Arousing,
Thunder

3. CHUN
Difficulty at the Beginning

THE JUDGEMENT

Difficulty at the Beginning
works supreme success,
Furthering through perseverance.
Nothing should be undertaken.
It furthers one to appoint helpers.

THE IMAGE

Clouds and thunder:
The image of Difficulty at the
Beginning.
Thus the superior man
Brings order out of confusion.

THE LINES

Nine at the beginning means:
Hesitation and hindrance.
It furthers one to remain
persevering.
It furthers one to appoint helpers.

Six in the second place means:
Difficulties pile up.
Horse and wagon part.
He is not a robber;
He wants to woo when the time
comes.
The maiden is chaste,
She does not pledge herself.
Ten years-then she pledges herself.

Six in the third place means:
Whoever hunts deer without the
forester
Only loses his way in the forest.
The superior man understands the
signs of the time
And prefers to desist.
To go on brings humiliation.

Six in the fourth place means:
Horse and wagon part.
Strive for union.
To go brings good fortune.
Everything acts to further.

Nine in the fifth place means:
Difficulties in blessing.
A little perseverance brings good
fortune.
Great perseverance brings
misfortune.

Six at the top means:
Horse and wagon part.
Bloody tears flow.

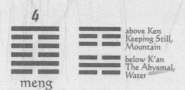

4

meng

above Kên
Keeping Still,
Mountain

below K'an
The Abysmal,
Water

4. MENG
Youthful Folly

THE JUDGEMENT

Youthful Folly has success.
It is not I who seek the young fool;
The young fool seeks me.
At the first oracle I inform him.
If he asks two or three times, it is
importunity.
If he importunes, I give him no
information.
Perseverance furthers.

THE IMAGE

A spring wells up at the foot of the
mountain:
The image of Youth.
Thus the superior man fosters his
character
By thoroughness in all that he does.

THE LINES

Six at the beginning means:
To make a fool develop
It furthers one to apply discipline.
The fetters should be removed.
To go on in this way brings
humiliation.

Nine in the second place means:
To bear with fools in kindliness
brings good fortune.
To know how to take women
Brings good fortune.
The son is capable of taking charge
of the household.

Six in the third place means:
Take not a maiden who, when she
sees a man of bronze,
Loses possession of herself.
Nothing furthers.

Six in the fourth place means:
Entangled folly brings humiliation.

Six in the fifth place means:
Childlike folly brings good fortune.

Nine at the top means:
In punishing folly
It does not further one
To commit transgressions.
The only thing that furthers
Is to prevent transgressions.

5

hsu

above K'an
The Abysmal,
Water

below Ch'ien
The Creative,
Heaven

5. HSU
Waiting (Nourishment)

THE JUDGEMENT

Waiting. If you are sincere,
You have light and success.
Perseverance brings good fortune.
It furthers one to cross the great
water.

THE IMAGE

Clouds rise up to heaven:
The image of Waiting.
Thus the superior man eats and
drinks,
Is joyous and of good cheer.

THE LINES

Nine at the beginning means:
Waiting in the meadow.
It furthers one to abide in what
endures.
No blame.

Nine in the second place means:
Waiting on the sand.
There is some gossip.
The end brings good fortune.

Nine in the third place means:
Waiting in the mud
Brings about the arrival of the
enemy.
Six in the fourth place means:
Waiting in blood.
Get out of the pit.

Nine in the fifth place means:
Waiting at meat and drink.
Perseverance brings good fortune.

Six at the top means:
One falls into the pit.
Three uninvited guests arrive.
Honor them, and in the end there
will be good fortune.

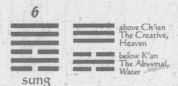

6

sung

above Ch'ien
The Creative,
Heaven

below K'an
The Abysmal,
Water

6. SUNG
Conflict of the Small

THE JUDGEMENT

Conflict. You are sincere
And are being obstructed.
A cautious halt halfway brings good
fortune.
Going through to the end brings
misfortune.
It furthers one to see the great man.
It does not further one to cross the
great water.

THE IMAGE

Heaven and water go their opposite
ways:
The image of Conflict.
Thus in all his transactions the
superior man
Carefully considers the beginning.

THE LINES

Six at the beginning means:
If one does not perpetuate the affair,
There is a little gossip.
In the end, good fortune comes.

Nine in the second place means:
One cannot engage in conflict;
One returns home, gives way.
The people of his town,
Three hundred households,
Remain free of guilt.

Six in the third place means:
To nourish oneself on ancient virtue
induces perseverance.
Danger. In the end, good fortune
comes.
If by chance you are in the service of
a king,
Seek not works.

Nine in the fourth place means:
One cannot engage in conflict.
One turns back and submits to fate,
Changes one's attitude,
And finds peace in perseverance.
Good fortune.

Nine in the fifth place means:
To contend before him
Brings supreme good fortune.

Nine at the top means:
Even if by chance a leather belt is
bestowed on one,
By the end of a morning
It will have been snatched away
three times.

7

above K'un
The Receptive,
Earth

below K'an
The Abysmal,
Water

shih

7. SHIH
The Army

THE JUDGEMENT

The Army. The army needs
perseverance
And a strong man.
Good fortune without blame.

THE IMAGE

In the middle of the earth is water:
The image of the Army.
Thus the superior man increases his
masses
By generosity toward the people.

THE LINES

Six at the beginning means:
An army must set forth in proper
order.
If the order is not good, misfortune
threatens.

Nine in the second place means:
In the midst of the army.
Good fortune. No blame.
The king bestows a triple
decoration.

Six in the third place means:
Perchance the army carries corpses
in the wagon.
Misfortune.

Six in the fourth place means:
The army retreats. No blame.

Six in the fifth place means:
There is game in the field.
It furthers one to catch it.
Without blame.
Let the eldest lead the army.
The younger transports corpses;
Then perseverance brings
misfortune.

Six at the top means:
The great prince issues commands,
Founds states, vests families with
fiefs.
Inferior people should not be
employed.

8

pi

above K'an
The Abysmal,
Water

below K'un
The Receptive,
Earth

8. PI
Holding Together [Union]

THE JUDGEMENT

Holding Together brings good
fortune.
Inquire of the oracle once again
Whether you possess sublimity,
constancy, and perseverance;
Then there is no blame.
Those who are uncertain gradually
join.
Whoever comes too late
Meets with misfortune.

THE IMAGE

On the earth is water:
The image of Holding Together.
Thus the kings of antiquity
Bestowed the different states as
fiefs
And cultivated friendly relations
With the feudal lords.

THE LINES

Six at the beginning means:
Hold to him in truth and loyalty;
This is without blame.
Truth, like a full earthen bowl:
Thus in the end
Good fortune comes from without.

Six in the second place means:
Hold to him inwardly.
Perseverance brings good fortune.

Six in the third place means:
You hold together with the wrong
people.

Six in the fourth place means:
Hold to him outwardly also.
Perseverance brings good fortune.

Nine in the fifth place means:
Manifestation of holding together.
In the hunt the king uses beaters on
three sides only
And foregoes game that runs off in
front.
The citizens need no warning.
Good fortune.

Six at the top means:
He finds no head for holding
together.
Misfortune.

9

hsiao ch'u

above Sun
The Gentle,
Wind

below Ch'ien
The Creative,
Heaven

9. HSIAO CH'U
The Taming Power of the Small

THE JUDGEMENT

The Taming Power of the Small
Has success.
Dense clouds, no rain from our
western region.

THE IMAGE

The wind drives across heaven:
The image of the Taming Power of
the Small.
Thus the superior man
Refines the outward aspect of his
nature.

THE LINES

Nine at the beginning means:
Return to the way.
How could there be blame in this?
Good fortune.

Nine in the second place means:
He allows himself to be drawn into
returning.
Good fortune.

Nine in the third place means:
The spokes burst out of the wagon
wheels.
Man and wife roll their eyes.

Six in the fourth place means:
If you are sincere, blood vanishes
and fear gives way.
No blame.

Nine in the fifth place means:
If you are sincere and loyally
attached,
You are rich in your neighbor.

Nine at the top means:
The rain comes, there is rest.
This is due to the lasting effect of
character.
Perseverance brings the woman into
danger.
The moon is nearly full.
If the superior man persists,
Misfortune comes.

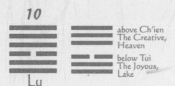

10

Lu

above Ch'ien
The Creative,
Heaven

below Tui
The Joyous,
Lake

10. LU
Treading [Conduct]

THE JUDGEMENT

Treading. Treading upon the tail of
the tiger.
It does not bite the man. Success.

THE IMAGE

Heaven above, the lake below:
The image of Treading.
Thus the superior man discriminates
between high and low,
And thereby fortifies the thinking of
the people.

THE LINES

Nine at the beginning means:
Simple conduct. Progress without
blame.

Nine in the second place means:
Treading a smooth, level course.
The perseverance of a dark man
Brings good fortune.

Six in the third place means:
A one-eyed man is able to see,
A lame man is able to tread.
He treads on the tail of the tiger.
The tiger bites the man.
Misfortune.
Thus does a warrior act on behalf of
his great prince.

Nine in the fourth place means:
He treads on the tail of the tiger.
Caution and circumspection
Lead ultimately to good fortune.

Nine in the fifth place means:
Resolute conduct.
Perseverance with awareness of
danger.

Nine at the top means:
Look to your conduct and weigh the
favorable signs.
When everything is fulfilled,
supreme good fortune comes.

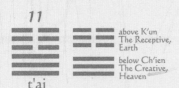

11

t'ai

above K'un
The Receptive,
Earth

below Ch'ien
The Creative,
Heaven

11. T'AI
Peace

THE JUDGEMENT

Peace. The small departs,
The great approaches.
Good fortune. Success.

THE IMAGE

Heaven and earth unite: the image
of Peace.
Thus the ruler
Divides and completes the course of
heaven and earth;
He furthers and regulates the gifts
of heaven and earth,
And so aids the people.

THE LINES

Nine at the beginning means:
When ribbon grass is pulled up, the
sod comes with it.
Each according to his kind.
Undertakings bring good fortune.

Nine in the second place means:
Bearing with the uncultured in
gentleness,
Fording the river with resolution,
Not neglecting what is distant,
Not regarding one's companions:
Thus one may manage to walk in
the middle.

Nine in the third place means:
No plain not followed by a slope.
No going not followed by a return.
He who remains persevering in
danger
Is without blame.
Do not complain about this truth;

Enjoy the good fortune you still
possess.

Six in the fourth place means:
He flutters down, not boasting of
his wealth,
Together with his neighbor,
Guileless and sincere.

Six in the fifth place means:
The sovereign I
Gives his daughter in marriage.
This brings blessing
And supreme good fortune.

Six at the top means:
The wall falls back into the moat.
Use no arm now.
Make your commands known
within your own town.
Perseverance brings humiliation.

12

p'i

above Ch'ien
The Creative,
Heaven

below K'un
The Receptive,
Earth

12. P'I
Standstill [Stagnation]

THE JUDGEMENT

Standstill. Evil people do not further
The perseverance of the superior
man.
The great departs; the small
approaches.

THE IMAGE

Heaven and earth do not unite:
The image of Standstill.
Thus the superior man falls back
upon his inner worth
In order to escape the difficulties.
He does not permit himself to be
honored with revenue.

THE LINES

Six at the beginning means:
When ribbon grass is pulled up, the
sod comes with it.
Each according to his kind.
Perseverance brings good fortune
and success.

Six in the second place means:
They bear and endure;
This means good fortune for inferior
people.
The standstill serves to help the
great man to attain success.

Six in the third place means:
They bear shame.

Nine in the fourth place means:
He who acts at the command of the
highest
Remains without blame.
Those of like mind partake of the
blessing.

Nine in the fifth place means:
Standstill is giving way.
Good fortune for the great man.
"What if it should fail, what if it
should fail?"
In this way he ties it to a cluster of
mulberry shoots.

Nine at the top means:
The standstill comes to an end.
First standstill, then good fortune.

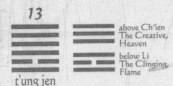

above Ch'ien
The Creative,
Heaven

below Li
The Clinging,
Flame

t'ung jen

13. T'UNG JEN
Fellowship with Men

THE JUDGEMENT

Fellowship with Men in the open.
Success.
It furthers one to cross the great
water.
The perseverance of the superior
man furthers.

THE IMAGE

Heaven together with fire:
The image of Fellowship with Men.
Thus the superior man organizes
the clans
And makes distinctions between
things.

THE LINES

Nine at the beginning means:
Fellowship with men at the gate.
No blame.

Six in the second place means:
Fellowship with men in the clan.
Humiliation.

Nine in the third place means:
He hides weapons in the thicket;
He climbs the high hill in front of
it.
For three years he does not rise up.

Nine in the fourth place means:
He climbs up on his wall; he cannot
attack.
Good fortune.

Nine in the fifth place means:
Men bound in fellowship first weep
and lament,
But afterward they laugh.
After great struggles they succeed
in meeting.

Nine at the top means:
Fellowship with men in the
meadow.
No remorse.

14

ta yu

above Li
The Clinging,
Flame

below Ch'ien
The Creative,
Heaven

14. TA YU
Possession in Great Measure

THE JUDGEMENT

Possession in Great Measure.
Supreme success.

THE IMAGE

Fire in heaven above:
The image of Possession in Great
Measure.
Thus the superior man curbs evil
and furthers good,
And thereby obeys the benevolent
will of heaven.

THE LINES

Nine at the beginning means:
No relationship with what is
harmful;
There is no blame in this.
If one remains conscious of
difficulty,
One remains without blame.

Nine in the second place means:
A big wagon for loading.
One may undertake something.
No blame.

Nine in the third place means:
A prince offers it to the Son of
Heaven.
A petty man cannot do this.

Nine in the fourth place means:
He makes a difference
Between himself and his neighbor.
No blame.

Six in the fifth place means:
He whose truth is accessible, yet
dignified,
Has good fortune.

Nine at the top means:
He is blessed by heaven.
Good fortune.
Nothing that does not further.

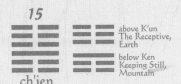

15
ch'ien

above K'un
The Receptive,
Earth

below Ken
Keeping Still,
Mountain

15. CH'IEN
Modesty

THE JUDGEMENT

Modesty creates success.
The superior man carries things
through.

THE IMAGE

Within the earth, a mountain:
The image of Modesty.
Thus the superior man reduces that
which is too much,
And augments that which is too
little.
He weighs things and makes them
equal.

THE LINES

Six at the beginning means:
A superior man modest about his
modesty
May cross the great water.
Good fortune.

Six in the second place means:
Modesty that comes to expression.
Perseverance brings good fortune.

Nine in the third place means:
A superior man of modesty and
merit
Carries things to conclusion.
Good fortune.

Six in the fourth place means:
Nothing that would not further
modesty
In movement.

Six in the fifth place means:
No boasting of wealth before one's
neighbor.
It is favorable to attack with force.
Nothing that would not further.

Six at the top means:
Modesty that comes to expression.
It is favorable to set armies
marching
To chastise one's own city and
one's country.

16

above Chen
The Arousing,
Thunder

below K'un
The Receptive,
Earth

yu

16. Yu
Enthusiasm

THE JUDGEMENT

Enthusiasm. It furthers one to
install helpers
And to set armies marching.

THE IMAGE

Thunder comes resounding out of
the earth:
The image of Enthusiasm.
Thus the ancient kings made music
In order to honor merit,
And offered it with splendor
To the Supreme Deity,
Inviting their ancestors to be
present.

THE LINES

Six at the beginning means:
Enthusiasm that expresses itself
Brings misfortune.

Six in the second place means:
Firm as a rock. Not a whole day.
Perseverance brings good fortune.

Six in the third place means:
Enthusiasm that looks upward
creates remorse.
Hesitation brings remorse.

Nine in the fourth place means:
The source of enthusiasm.
He achieves great things.
Doubt not.
You gather friends around you
As a hair clasp gathers the hair.

Six in the fifth place means:
Persistently ill, and still does not
die.

Six at the top means:
Deluded enthusiasm.
But if after completion one changes,
There is no blame.

above Tui
The Joyous,
Lake

below Chen
The Arousing,
Thunder

sui

17. SUI
Following

THE JUDGEMENT

Following has supreme success.
Perseverance furthers. No blame.

THE IMAGE

Thunder in the middle of the lake:
The image of Following.
Thus the superior man at nightfall
Goes indoors for rest and
recuperation.

THE LINES

Nine at the beginning means:
The standard is changing.
Perseverance brings good fortune.
To go out of the door in company
Produces deeds.

Six in the second place means:
If one clings to the little boy,
One loses the strong man.

Six in the third place means:
If one clings to the strong man,
One loses the little boy.
Through following one finds what
one seeks.
It furthers one to remain
persevering.

Nine in the fourth place means:
Following creates success.
Perseverance brings misfortune.
To go one's way with sincerity
brings clarity.
How could there be blame in this?

Nine in the fifth place means:
Sincere in the good. Good fortune.

Six at the top means:
He meets with firm allegiance
And is still further bound.
The king introduces him
To the Western Mountain.

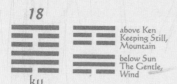

18

ku

above Ken
Keeping Still,
Mountain

below Sun
The Gentle,
Wind

18. KU
Work on What Has Been Spoiled [Decay]

THE JUDGEMENT

Work on What Has Been Spoiled
Has supreme success.
It furthers one to cross the great
water.
Before the starting point, three
days.
After the starting point, three days.

THE IMAGE

The wind blows low on the
mountain:
The image of Decay.
Thus the superior man stirs up the
people
And strengthens their spirit.

THE LINES

Six at the beginning means:
Setting right what has been spoiled
by the father.
If there is a son,
No blame rests upon the departed
father.
Danger. In the end good fortune.

Nine in the second place means:
Setting right what has been spoiled
by the mother.
One must not be too persevering.

Nine in the third place means:
Setting right what has been spoiled
by the father.
There will be little remorse.
No great blame.

Six in the fourth place means:
Tolerating what has been spoiled by
the father.
In continuing one sees humiliation.

Six in the fifth place means:
Setting right what has been spoiled
by the father.
One meets with praise.

Nine at the top means:
He does not serve kings and
princes,
Sets himself higher goals.

above K'un
The Receptive,
Earth

below Tui
The Joyous,
Lake

19. LIN
Approach

THE JUDGEMENT

Approach has supreme success.
Perseverance furthers.
When the eighth month comes,
There will be misfortune.

THE IMAGE

The earth above the lake:
The image of Approach.
Thus the superior man is
inexhaustible
In his will to teach,
And without limits
In his tolerance and protection of the
people.

THE LINES

Nine at the beginning means:
Joint approach.
Perseverance brings good fortune.

Nine in the second place means:
Joint approach.
Good fortune.
Everything furthers.

Six in the third place means:
Comfortable approach.
Nothing that would further.
If one is induced to grieve over it,
One becomes free of blame.

Six in the fourth place means:
Complete approach.
No blame.

Six in the fifth place means:
Wise approach.
This is right for a great prince.
Good fortune.

Six at the top means:
Greathearted approach.
Good fortune. No blame.

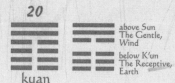

above Sun
The Gentle,
Wind

below K'un
The Receptive,
Earth

kuan

20. KUAN
Contemplation (View)

THE JUDGEMENT

Contemplation. The ablution has
been made,
But not yet the offering.
Full of trust they look up to him.

THE IMAGE

The wind blows over the earth:
The image of Contemplation.
Thus the kings of old visited the
regions of the world,
Contemplated the people,
And gave them instruction.

THE LINES

Six at the beginning means:
Boylike contemplation.
For an inferior man, no blame.
For a superior man, humiliation.

Six in the second place means:
Contemplation through the crack of
the door.
Furthering for the perseverance of a
woman.

Six in the third place means:
Contemplation of my life
Decides the choice
Between advance and retreat.

Six in the fourth place means:
Contemplation of the light of the
kingdom.
It furthers one to exert influence as
the guest of a king.

Nine in the fifth place means:
Contemplation of my life.
The superior man is without blame.

Nine at the top means:
Contemplation of his life.
The superior man is without blame.

21

shih ho

above Li
The Clinging,
Flame

below Chen
The Arousing,
Thunder

21. SHIH HO
Biting Through

THE JUDGEMENT

Biting Through has success.
It is favorable to let justice be
administered.

THE IMAGE

Thunder and lightning:
The image of Biting Through.
Thus the kings of former times made
firm the laws
Through clearly defined penalties.

THE LINES

Nine at the beginning means:
His feet are fastened in the stocks,
So that his toes disappear.
No blame.

Six in the second place means:
Bites through tender meat,
So that his nose disappears.
No blame.

Six in the third place means:
Bites on old dried meat
And strikes on something
poisonous.
Slight humiliation. No blame.

Nine in the fourth place means:
Bites on dried gristly meat.
Receives metal arrows.
It furthers one to be mindful of
difficulties
And to be persevering.
Good fortune.

Six in the fifth place means:
Bites on dried lean meat.
Receives yellow gold.
Perseveringly aware of danger.
No blame.

Nine at the top means:
His neck is fastened in the wooden
cangue,
So that his ears disappear.
Misfortune.

22

above Ken
Keeping Still,
Mountain

below Li
The Clinging,
Flame

pi

22. Pi
Grace

The Judgement

Grace has success.
In small matters
It is favorable to undertake
something.

The Image

Fire at the foot of the mountain:
The image of Grace.
Thus does the superior man proceed
When clearing up current affairs.
But he dare not decide controversial
issues in this way.

The Lines

Nine at the beginning means:
He lends grace to his toes, leaves
the carriage, and walks.

Six in the second place means:
Lends grace to the beard on his
chin.

Nine in the third place means:
Graceful and moist.
Constant perseverance brings good
fortune.

Six in the fourth place means:
Grace or simplicity?
A white horse comes as if on wings.
He is not a robber,
He will woo at the right time.

Six in the fifth place means:
Grace in hills and gardens.
The roll of silk is meager and small.
Humiliation, but in the end good
fortune.

Nine at the top means:
Simple grace. No blame.

above Ken
Keeping Still,
Mountain

below K'un
The Receptive,
Earth

23. PO
Splitting Apart

THE JUDGEMENT

 Splitting Apart. It does not further
one
To go anywhere.

THE IMAGE

The mountain rests on the earth:
The image of Splitting Apart.
Thus those above can ensure their
position
Only by giving generously to those
below.

THE LINES

Six at the beginning means:
The leg of the bed is split.
Those who persevere are destroyed.
Misfortune.

Six in the second place means:
The bed is split at the edge.
Those who persevere are destroyed.
Misfortune.

Six in the third place means:
He splits with them. No blame.

Six in the fourth place means:
The bed is split up to the skin.
Misfortune.

Six in the fifth place means:
A shoal of fishes. Favour comes
through the court ladies.
Everything acts to further.

Nine at the top means:
There is a large fruit still uneaten.
The superior man receives a
carriage.
The house of the inferior man is
split apart.

above K'un
The Receptive,
Earth

below Chen
The Arousing,
Thunder

fu

24. FU
Return (The Turning Point)

THE JUDGEMENT

Return. Success.
Going out and coming in without
error.
Friends come without blame.
To and fro goes the way.
On the seventh day comes return.
It furthers one to have somewhere to
go.

THE IMAGE

Thunder within the earth:
The image of the Turning Point.
Thus the kings of antiquity closed
the passes
At the time of solstice.
Merchants and strangers did not go
about,
And the ruler
Did not travel through the
provinces.

THE LINES

Nine at the beginning means:
Return from a short distance.
No need for remorse.
Great good fortune.

Six in the second place means:
Quiet return. Good fortune.

Six in the third place means:
Repeated return. Danger. No blame.

Six in the fourth place means:
Walking in the midst of others,
One returns alone.

Six in the fifth place means:
Noblehearted return. No remorse.

Six at the top means:
Missing the return. Misfortune.
Misfortune from within and
without.
If armies are set marching in this
way,
One will in the end suffer a great
defeat,
Disastrous for the ruler of the
country.
For ten years
It will not be possible to attack
again.

above Ch'ien
The Creative,
Heaven

below Chen
The Arousing,
Thunder

25. WU WANG
Innocence (The Unexpected)

THE JUDGEMENT

Innocence. Supreme success.
Perseverance furthers.
If someone is not as he should be,
He has misfortune,
And it does not further him
To undertake anything.

THE IMAGE

Under heaven thunder rolls:
All things attain the natural state
of innocence.
Thus the kings of old,
 Rich in virtue, and in harmony
with the time,
Fostered and nourished all beings.

THE LINES

Nine at the beginning means:
Innocent behavior brings good
fortune.

Six in the second place means:
If one does not count on the harvest
while plowing,
Nor on the use of the ground while
clearing it,
It furthers one to undertake
something.

Six in the third place means:
Undeserved misfortune.
The cow that was tethered by
someone
Is the wanderer's gain, the citizen's
loss.

Nine in the fourth place means:
He who can be persevering
Remains without blame.

Nine in the fifth place means:
Use no medicine in an illness
Incurred through no fault of your
own.
It will pass of itself.

Nine at the top means:
Innocent action brings misfortune.
Nothing furthers.

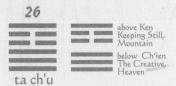

above Ken
Keeping Still,
Mountain

below Ch'ien
The Creative,
Heaven

ta ch'u

26. TA CH'U
The Taming Power of the Great

THE JUDGEMENT

The Taming Power of the Great.
Perseverance furthers.
Not eating at home brings good
fortune.
It furthers one to cross the great
water.

THE IMAGE

Heaven within the mountain:
The image of the Taming Power of
the Great.
Thus the superior man acquaints
himself with many sayings of
antiquity
And many deeds of the past,
In order to strengthen his character
thereby.

THE LINES

Nine at the beginning means:
Danger is at hand. It furthers one to
desist.

Nine in the second place means:
The axletrees are taken from the
wagon.

Nine in the third place means:
A good horse that follows others.
Awareness of danger,
With perseverance, furthers.
Practice chariot driving and armed
defense daily.
It furthers one to have somewhere to
go.

Six in the fourth place means:
The headboard of a young bull.
Great good fortune.

Six in the fifth place means:
The tusk of a gelded boar.
Good fortune.

Nine at the top means:
One attains the way of heaven.
Success.

above Ken
Keeping Still,
Mountain

below Chen
The Arousing,
Thunder

27. I
Providing Nourishment

THE JUDGEMENT

The Corners of the Mouth.
Perseverance brings good fortune.
Pay heed to the providing of
nourishment
And to what a man seeks
To fill his own mouth with.

THE IMAGE

At the foot of the mountain,
thunder:
The image of Providing
Nourishment.
Thus the superior man is careful of
his words
And temperate in eating and
drinking.

THE LINES

Nine at the beginning means:
You let your magic tortoise go,
And look at me with the corners of
your mouth drooping.
Misfortune.

Six in the second place means:
Turning to the summit for
nourishment,
Deviating from the path
To seek nourishment from the hill.
Continuing to do this brings
misfortune.

Six in the third place means:
Turning away from nourishment.
Perseverance brings misfortune.
Do not act thus for ten years.
Nothing serves to further.

Six in the fourth place means:
Turning to the summit
For provision of nourishment
Brings good fortune.
Spying about with sharp eyes
Like a tiger with insatiable craving.
No blame.

Six in the fifth place means:
Turning away from the path.
To remain persevering brings good
fortune.
One should not cross the great
water.

Nine at the top means:
The source of nourishment.
Awareness of danger brings good
fortune.
It furthers one to cross the great
water.

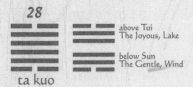

above Tui
The Joyous, Lake

below Sun
The Gentle, Wind

ta kuo

28. TA KUO
Preponderance of the Great

THE JUDGEMENT

Preponderance of the Great.
The ridgepole sags to the breaking
point.
It furthers one to have somewhere to
go.
Success.

THE IMAGE

The lake rises above the trees:
The image of Preponderance of the
Great.
Thus the superior man, when he
stands alone,
Is unconcerned,
And if he has to renounce the world,
He is undaunted.

THE LINES

Six at the beginning means:
To spread white rushes underneath.
No blame.

Nine in the second place means:
A dry poplar sprouts at the root.
An older man takes a young wife.
Everything furthers.

Nine in the third place means:
The ridgepole sags to the breaking
point.
Misfortune.

Nine in the fourth place means:
The ridgepole is braced. Good
fortune.
If there are ulterior motives, it is
humiliating.

Nine in the fifth place means:
A withered poplar puts forth
flowers.
An older woman takes a husband.
No blame. No praise.

Six at the top means:
One must go through the water.
It goes over one's head.
Misfortune. No blame.

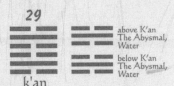

29

k'an

above K'an
The Abysmal,
Water

below K'an
The Abysmal,
Water

29. KA'N
The Abysmal (Water)

THE JUDGEMENT

The Abysmal repeated.
If you are sincere, you have success
in your heart,
And whatever you do succeeds.

THE IMAGE

Water flows on uninterruptedly and
reaches its goal:
The image of the Abysmal
repeated.
Thus the superior man walks in
lasting virtue
And carries on the business of
teaching.

THE LINES

Six at the beginning means:
Repetition of the Abysmal.
In the abyss one falls into a pit.
Misfortune.

Nine in the second place means:
The abyss is dangerous.
One should strive to attain small
things only.

Six in the third place means:
Forward and backward, abyss on
abyss.
In danger like this, pause at first
and wait,
Otherwise you will fall into a pit in
the abyss.
Do not act in this way.

Six in the fourth place means:
A jug of wine, a bowl of rice with it;
Earthen vessels
Simply handed in through the
window.
There is certainly no blame in this.

Nine in the fifth place means:
The abyss is not filled to
overflowing,
It is filled only to the rim.
No blame.

Six at the top means:
Bound with cords and ropes,
Shut in between thorn-hedged
prison walls:
For three years one does not find the
way.
Misfortune.

li

above Li
The Clinging,
Flame

below Li
The Clinging,
Flame

30. LI
The Clinging, Fire

THE JUDGEMENT

The Clinging. Perseverance furthers.
It brings success.
Care of the cow brings good fortune.

THE IMAGE

That which is bright rises twice:
The image of Fire.
Thus the great man, by perpetuating
this brightness,
Illumines the four quarters of the
world.

THE LINES

Nine at the beginning means:
The footprints run crisscross.
If one is seriously intent, no blame.

Six in the second place means:
Yellow light. Supreme good fortune.

Nine in the third place means:
In the light of the setting sun,
Men either beat the pot and sing
Or loudly bewail the approach of old
age.
Misfortune.

Nine in the fourth place means:
Its coming is sudden;
It flames up, dies down, is thrown
away.

Six in the fifth place means:
Tears in floods, sighing and
lamenting.
Good fortune.

Nine at the top means:
The king uses him to march forth
and chastise.
Then it is best to kill the leaders
And take captive the followers. No
blame.

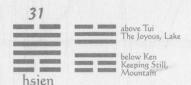

above Tui
The Joyous, Lake

below Ken
Keeping Still,
Mountain

hsien

31. HSIEN
Influence (Wooing)

THE JUDGEMENT

Influence. Success.
Perseverance furthers.
To take a maiden to wife brings
good fortune.

THE IMAGE

A lake on the mountain:
The image of Influence.
Thus the superior man encourages
people to approach him
By his readiness to receive them.

THE LINES

Six at the beginning means:
The influence shows itself in the big
toe.

Six in the second place means:
The influence shows itself in the
calves of the legs.
Misfortune.
Tarrying brings good fortune.

Nine in the third place means:
The influence shows itself in the
thighs.
Holds to that which follows it.
To continue is humiliating.

Nine in the fourth place means:
Perseverance brings good fortune.
Remorse disappears.
If a man is agitated in mind,
And his thoughts go hither and
thither,
Only those friends
On whom he fixes his conscious
thoughts
Will follow.

Nine in the fifth place means:
The influence shows itself in the
back of the neck.
No remorse.

Six at the top means:
The influence shows itself in the
jaws, cheeks, and tongue.

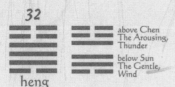

above Chen
The Arousing,
Thunder

below Sun
The Gentle,
Wind

heng

32. HENG
Duration

THE JUDGEMENT

Duration. Success. No blame.
Perseverance furthers.
It furthers one to have somewhere to
go.

THE IMAGE

Thunder and wind: the image of
Duration.
Thus the superior man stands firm
And does not change his direction.

THE LINES

Six at the beginning means:
Seeking duration too hastily brings
misfortune persistently.
Nothing that would further.

Nine in the second place means:
Remorse disappears.

Nine in the third place means:
He who does not give duration to
his character
Meets with disgrace.
Persistent humiliation.

Nine in the fourth place means:
No game in the field.

Six in the fifth place means:
Giving duration to one's character
through perseverance.
This is good fortune for a woman,
misfortune for a man.

Six at the top means:
Restlessness as an enduring
condition brings misfortune.

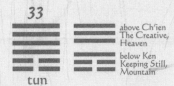

33

tun

above Ch'ien
The Creative,
Heaven

below Kên
Keeping Still,
Mountain

33. TUN
Retreat

THE JUDGEMENT

Retreat. Success.
In what is small, perseverance
furthers.

THE IMAGE

Mountain under heaven: the image
of Retreat.
Thus the superior man keeps the
inferior man at a distance,
Not angrily but with reserve.

THE LINES

Six at the beginning means:
 At the tail in retreat. This is
dangerous.
One must not wish to undertake
anything.

Six in the second place means:
He holds him fast with yellow
oxhide.
No one can tear him loose.

Nine in the third place means:
A halted retreat
Is nerve-wracking and dangerous.
To retain people as men—and
maidservants
Brings good fortune.

Nine in the fourth place means:
Voluntary retreat brings good
fortune to the superior man
And downfall to the inferior man.

Nine in the fifth place means:
Friendly retreat. Perseverance
brings good fortune.

Nine at the top means:
Cheerful retreat. Everything serves
to further.

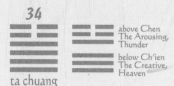

above Chen
The Arousing,
Thunder

below Ch'ien
The Creative,
Heaven

ta chuang

34. TA CHUANG
The Power of the Great

THE JUDGEMENT

The Power of the Great.
Perseverance furthers.

THE IMAGE

Thunder in heaven above:
The image of the Power of the
Great.
Thus the superior man does not
tread upon paths
That do not accord with established
order.

THE LINES

Nine at the beginning means:
Power in the toes.
Continuing brings misfortune.
This is certainly true.

Nine in the second place means:
Perseverance brings good fortune.

Nine in the third place means:
The inferior man works through
power.
The superior man does not act thus.
To continue is dangerous.
A goat butts against a hedge
And gets its horns entangled.

Nine in the fourth place means:
Perseverance brings good fortune.
Remorse disappears.
The hedge opens; there is no
entanglement.
Power depends upon the axle of a
big cart.

Six in the fifth place means:
Loses the goat with ease.
No remorse.

Six at the top means:
A goat butts against a hedge.
It cannot go backward, it cannot go
forward.
Nothing serves to further.
If one notes the difficulty, this
brings good fortune.

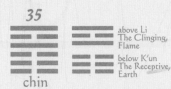

above Li
The Clinging,
Flame

below K'un
The Receptive,
Earth

chin

35. CHIN
Progress

THE JUDGEMENT

Progress. The powerful prince
Is honored with horses in large
numbers.
In a single day he is granted
audience three times.

THE IMAGE

The sun rises over the earth:
The image of Progress.
Thus the superior man himself
Brightens his bright virtue.

THE LINES

Six at the beginning means:
Progressing, but turned back.
Perseverance brings good fortune.
If one meets with no confidence,
one should remain calm.
No mistake.

Six in the second place means:
Progressing, but in sorrow.
Perseverance brings good fortune.
Then one obtains great happiness
from one's ancestress.

Six in the third place means:
All are in accord. Remorse
disappears.

Nine in the fourth place means:
Progress like a hamster.
Perseverance brings danger.

Six in the fifth place means:
Remorse disappears.
Take not gain and loss to heart.
Undertakings bring good fortune.
Everything serves to further.

Nine at the top means:
Making progress with the horns is
permissible
Only for the purpose of punishing
one's own city.
To be conscious of danger brings
good fortune.
No blame.
Perseverance brings humiliation.

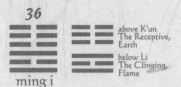

above K'un
The Receptive,
Earth

below Li
The Clinging,
Flame

36. MING I
Darkening of the Light

THE JUDGEMENT

Darkening of the Light. In adversity
It furthers one to be persevering.

THE IMAGE

The light has sunk into the earth:
The image of Darkening of the
Light.
Thus does the superior man live
with the great mass:
He veils his light, yet still shines.

THE LINES

Nine at the beginning means:
Darkening of the light during flight.
He lowers his wings.
The superior man does not eat for
three days
On his wanderings.
But he has somewhere to go.
The host has occasion to gossip
about him.

Six in the second place means:
Darkening of the light injures him in
the left thigh.
He gives aid with the strength of a
horse.
Good fortune.

Nine in the third place means:
Darkening of the light during the
hunt in the south.
Their great leader is captured.
One must not expect perseverance
too soon.

Six in the fourth place means:
He penetrates the left side of the
belly.
One gets at the very heart of the
darkening of the light,
And leaves gate and courtyard.

Six in the fifth place means:
Darkening of the light as with
Prince Chi.
Perseverance furthers.

Six at the top means:
Not light but darkness.
First he climbed up to heaven,
Then he plunged into the depths of
the earth.

above Sun
The Gentle,
Wind

below Li
The Clinging,
Flame

37. CHIA JEN
The Family [The Clan]

THE JUDGEMENT

The Family. The perseverance of the
woman furthers.

THE IMAGE

Wind comes forth from fire:
The image of the Family.
Thus the superior man has
substance in his words
And duration in his way of life.

THE LINES

Nine at the beginning means:
Firm seclusion within the family.
Remorse disappears.

Six in the second place means:
She should not follow her whims.
She must attend within to the food.
Perseverance brings good fortune.

Nine in the third place means:
When tempers flare up in the
family,
Too great severity brings remorse.
Good fortune nonetheless.
When woman and child dally and
laugh,
It leads in the end to humiliation.

Six in the fourth place means:
She is the treasure of the house.
Great good fortune.

Nine in the fifth place means:
As a king he approaches his family.
Fear not.
Good fortune.

Nine at the top means:
His work commands respect.
In the end good fortune comes.

38

k'uei

above Li
The Clinging,
Flame

below Tui
The Joyous,
Lake

38. K'UEI
Opposition

The Judgement

Opposition. In small matters, good
fortune.

The Image

Above, fire; below, the lake:
The image of Opposition.
Thus amid all fellowship
The superior man retains his
individuality.

The Lines

Nine at the beginning means:
Remorse disappears.
If you lose your horse, do not run
after it;
It will come back of its own accord.
When you see evil people,
Guard yourself against mistakes.

Nine in the second place means:
One meets his lord in a narrow
street.
No blame.

Six in the third place means:
One sees the wagon dragged back,
The oxen halted,
A man's hair and nose cut off.
Not a good beginning, but a good
end.

Nine in the fourth place means:
Isolated through opposition,
One meets a like-minded man
With whom one can associate in
good faith.
Despite the danger, no blame.

Six in the fifth place means:
Remorse disappears.
The companion bites his way
through the wrappings.
If one goes to him,
How could it be a mistake?

Nine at the top means:
Isolated through opposition,
One sees one's companion as a pig
covered with dirt,
As a wagon full of devils.
First one draws a bow against him,
Then one lays the bow aside.
He is not a robber; he will woo at
the right time.
As one goes, rain falls; then good
fortune comes.

above K'an
The Abysmal,
Water

below Ken
Keeping Still,
Mountain

chien

39. CHIEN
Obstruction

THE JUDGEMENT

Obstruction. The southwest
furthers.
The northeast does not further.
It furthers one to see the great man.
Perseverance brings good fortune.

THE IMAGE

Water on the mountain:
The image of Obstruction.
Thus the superior man turns his
attention to himself
And molds his character.

THE LINES

Six at the beginning means:
Going leads to obstructions,
Coming meets with praise.

Six in the second place means:
The king's servant is beset by
obstruction upon obstruction,
But it is not his own fault.

Nine in the third place means:
Going leads to obstructions;
Hence he comes back.

Six in the fourth place means:
Going leads to obstructions,
Coming leads to union.

Nine in the fifth place means:
In the midst of the greatest
obstructions,
Friends come.

Six at the top means:
Going leads to obstructions,
Coming leads to great good
fortune.
It furthers one to see the great man.

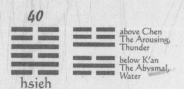

hsieh

above Chen
The Arousing,
Thunder

below K'an
The Abysmal,
Water

40. HSIEH
Deliverance

THE JUDGEMENT

Deliverance. The southwest
furthers.
If there is no longer anything where
one has to go,
Return brings good fortune.
If there is still something where one
has to go,
Hastening brings good fortune.

THE IMAGE

Thunder and rain set in:
The image of Deliverance.
Thus the superior man pardons
mistakes
And forgives misdeeds.

THE LINES

Six at the beginning means:
Without blame.

Nine in the second place means:
One kills three foxes in the field
And receives a yellow arrow.
Perseverance brings good fortune.

Six in the third place means:
If a man carries a burden on his back
And nonetheless rides in a carriage,
He thereby encourages robbers to
draw near.
Perseverance leads to humiliation.

Nine in the fourth place means:
Deliver yourself from your great toe.
Then the companion comes,
And him you can trust.

Six in the fifth place means:
If only the superior man can deliver
himself,
It brings good fortune.
Thus he proves to inferior men that
he is in earnest.

Six at the top means:
The prince shoots at a hawk on a
high wall.
He kills it. Everything serves to
further.

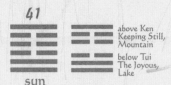

41

sun

above Ken
Keeping Still,
Mountain

below Tui
The Joyous,
Lake

41. SUN
Decrease

THE JUDGEMENT

Decrease combined with sincerity
Brings about supreme good fortune
Without blame.
One may be persevering in this.
It furthers one to undertake
something.
How is this to be carried out?
One may use two small bowls for
the sacrifice.

THE IMAGE

At the foot of the mountain, the
lake:
The image of Decrease.
Thus the superior man controls his
anger
And restrains his instincts.

THE LINES

Nine at the beginning means:
Going quickly when one's tasks are
finished
Is without blame.
But one must reflect on how much
one may decrease others.

Nine in the second place means:
Perseverance furthers.
To undertake something brings
misfortune.
Without decreasing oneself,
One is able to bring increase to
others.

Six in the third place means:
When three people journey together,
Their number decreases by one.
When one man journeys alone,
He finds a companion.

Six in the fourth place means:
If a man decreases his faults,
It makes the other hasten to come
and rejoice.
No blame.

Six in the fifth place means:
Someone does indeed increase him.
Ten pairs of tortoises cannot oppose
it.
Supreme good fortune.

Nine at the top means:
If one is increased without
depriving others,
There is no blame.
Perseverance brings good fortune.
It furthers one to undertake
something.
One obtains servants But no longer
has a separate home.

42

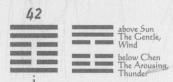

above Sun
The Gentle,
Wind

below Chen
The Arousing,
Thunder

i

42. 1
Increase

THE JUDGEMENT

Increase. It furthers one
To undertake something.
It furthers one to cross the great
water.

THE IMAGE

Wind and thunder: the image of
Increase.
Thus the superior man:
If he sees good, he imitates it;
If he has faults, he rids himself of
them.

THE LINES

Nine at the beginning means:
It furthers one to accomplish great
deeds.
Supreme good fortune. No blame.

Six in the second place means:
Someone does indeed increase him;
Ten pairs of tortoises cannot oppose
it.
Constant perseverance brings good
fortune.
The king presents him before God.
Good fortune.

Six in the third place means:
One is enriched through unfortunate
events.
No blame, if you are sincere
And walk in the middle,
And report with a seal to the prince.

Six in the fourth place means:
If you walk in the middle
And report to the prince,
He will follow.
It furthers one to be used
In the removal of the capital.

Nine in the fifth place means:
If in truth you have a kind heart, ask
not.
Supreme good fortune.
Truly, kindness will be recognized as
your virtue.

Nine at the top means:
He brings increase to no one.
Indeed, someone even strikes him.
He does not keep his heart
constantly steady.
Misfortune.

43

kuai

above Tui
The Joyous,
Lake

below Ch'ien
The Creative,
Heaven

43. KUAI
Break-through (Resoluteness)

THE JUDGEMENT

Break-through. One must resolutely
make the matter known
At the court of the king.
It must be announced truthfully.
Danger.
It is necessary to notify one's own
city.
It does not further to resort to arms.
It furthers one to undertake
something.

THE IMAGE

The lake has risen up to heaven:
The image of Break-through.
Thus the superior man
Dispenses riches downward
And refrains from resting on his
virtue.

THE LINES

Nine at the beginning means:
Mighty in the forward-striding
toes.
When one goes and is not equal to
the task,
One makes a mistake.

Nine in the second place means:
A cry of alarm. Arms at evening
and at night.
Fear nothing.

Nine in the third place means:
To be powerful in the cheekbones
Brings misfortune.
The superior man is firmly resolved.
He walks alone and is caught in the
rain.
He is bespattered,
And people murmur against him.
No blame.

Nine in the fourth place means:
There is no skin on his thighs,
And walking comes hard.
If a man were to let himself be led
like a sheep,
Remorse would disappear.
But if these words are heard
They will not be believed.

Nine in the fifth place means:
In dealing with weeds,
Firm resolution is necessary.
Walking in the middle
Remains free of blame.

Six at the top means:
No cry.
In the end misfortune comes.

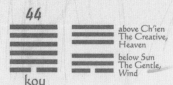

above Ch'ien
The Creative,
Heaven

below Sun
The Gentle,
Wind

kou

44. KOU
Coming to Meet

THE JUDGEMENT

Coming to Meet. The maiden is
powerful.
One should not marry such a
maiden.

THE IMAGE

Under heaven, wind:
The image of Coming to Meet.
Thus does the prince act when
disseminating his commands
And proclaiming them to the four
quarters of heaven.

THE LINES

Six at the beginning means:
It must be checked with a brake of
bronze.
Perseverance brings good fortune.
If one lets it take its course, one
experiences misfortune.
Even a lean pig has it in him to rage
around.

Nine in the second place means:
There is a fish in the tank. No
blame.
Does not further guests.

Nine in the third place means:
There is no skin on his thighs,
And walking comes hard.
If one is mindful of the danger,
No great mistake is made.

Nine in the fourth place means:
No fish in the tank.
This leads to misfortune.

Nine in the fifth place means:
A melon covered with willow leaves.
Hidden lines.
Then it drops down to one from
heaven.

Nine at the top means:
He comes to meet with his horns.
Humiliation. No blame.

ts'ui

above Tui
The Joyous,
Lake

below K'un
The Receptive,
Earth

45. Ts'ui
Gathering Together [Massing]

THE JUDGEMENT

Gathering Together. Success.
The king approaches his temple.
It furthers one to see the great man.
This brings success. Perseverance
furthers.
To bring great offerings creates
good fortune.
It furthers one to undertake
something.

THE IMAGE

Over the earth, the lake:
The image of Gathering Together.
Thus the superior man renews his
weapons
In order to meet the unforeseen.

THE LINES

Six at the beginning means:
If you are sincere, but not to the
end,
There will sometimes be confusion,
sometimes gathering together.
If you call out,
Then after one grasp of the hand
you can laugh again.
Regret not. Going is without
blame.

Six in the second place means:
Letting oneself be drawn
Brings good fortune and remains
blameless.
If one is sincere,
It furthers one to bring even a small
offering.

Six in the third place means:
Gathering together amid sighs.
Nothing that would further.
Going is without blame.
Slight humiliation.

Nine in the fourth place means:
Great good fortune. No blame.

Nine in the fifth place means:
If in gathering together one has
position,
This brings no blame.
If there are some who are not yet
sincerely in the work,
Sublime and enduring perseverance
is needed.
Then remorse disappears.

Six at the top means:
Lamenting and sighing, floods of
tears. No blame.

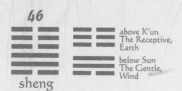

sheng

above K'un
The Receptive,
Earth

below Sun
The Gentle,
Wind

46. SHENG
Pushing Upward

THE JUDGEMENT

Pushing Upward has supreme
success.
One must see the great man.
Fear not.
Departure toward the south
Brings good fortune.

THE IMAGE

Within the earth, wood grows:
The image of Pushing Upward.
Thus the superior man of devoted
character
Heaps up small things
In order to achieve something high
and great.

THE LINES

Six at the beginning means:
Pushing upward that meets with
confidence
Brings great good fortune.

Nine in the second place means:
If one is sincere,
It furthers one to bring even a small
offering.
No blame.

Nine in the third place means:
One pushes upward into an empty
city.

Six in the fourth place means:
The king offers him Mount Ch'i.
Good fortune. No blame.

Six in the fifth place means:
Perseverance brings good fortune.
One pushes upward by steps.

Six at the top means:
Pushing upward in darkness.
It furthers one
To be unremittingly persevering.

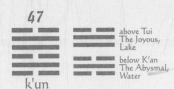

47

above Tui
The Joyous,
Lake

below K'an
The Abysmal,
Water

k'un

47. K'UN
Oppression (Exhaustion)

THE JUDGEMENT

Oppression. Success. Perseverance.
The great man brings about good
fortune.
No blame.
When one has something to say,
It is not believed.

THE IMAGE

There is no water in the lake:
The image of Exhaustion.
Thus the superior man stakes his
life
On following his will.

THE LINES

Six at the beginning means:
One sits oppressed under a bare
tree
And strays into a gloomy valley.
For three years one sees nothing.

Nine in the second place means:
One is oppressed while at meat and
drink.
The man with the scarlet knee
bands is just coming.
It furthers one to offer sacrifice.
To set forth brings misfortune.
No blame.

Six in the third place means:
A man permits himself to be
oppressed by stone,
And leans on thorns and thistles.
He enters his house and does not
see his wife.
Misfortune.

Nine in the fourth place means:
He comes very quietly, oppressed in
a golden carriage.
Humiliation, but the end is reached.

Nine in the fifth place means:
His nose and feet are cut off.
Oppression at the hands of the man
with the purple knee bands.
Joy comes softly.
It furthers one to make offerings
and libations.

Six at the top means:
He is oppressed by creeping vines.
He moves uncertainly and says,
"Movement brings remorse."
If one feels remorse over this and
makes a start,
Good fortune comes.

48

ching

above K'an
The Abysmal,
Water

below Sun
The Gentle,
Wind

48. CHING
The Well

THE JUDGEMENT

The Well. The town may be
changed,
But the well cannot be changed.
It neither decreases nor increases.
They come and go and draw from
the well.
If one gets down almost to the water
And the rope does not go all the
way,
Or the jug breaks, it brings
misfortune.

THE IMAGE

Water over wood: the image of the
Well.
Thus the superior man encourages
the people at their work,
And exhorts them to help one
another.

THE LINES

Six at the beginning means:
One does not drink the mud of the
well.
No animals come to an old well.

Nine in the second place means:
At the wellhole one shoots fishes.
The jug is broken and leaks.

Nine in the third place means:
The well is cleaned, but no one
drinks from it.
This is my heart's sorrow,
For one might draw from it.
If the king were clear-minded,
Good fortune might be enjoyed in
common.

Six in the fourth place means:
The well is being lined. No blame.

Nine in the fifth place means:
In the well there is a clear, cold
spring
From which one can drink.

Six at the top means:
One draws from the well
Without hindrance.
It is dependable.
Supreme good fortune.

above Tui
The Joyous,
Lake

below Li
The Clinging,
Flame

ko

49. KO
Revolution (Molting)

THE JUDGEMENT

Revolution. On your own day
You are believed.
Supreme success,
Furthering through perseverance.
Remorse disappears.

THE IMAGE

Fire in the lake: the image of
Revolution.
Thus the superior man
Sets the calendar in order
And makes the seasons clear.

THE LINES

Nine at the beginning means:
Wrapped in the hide of a yellow
cow.

Six in the second place means:
When one's own day comes, one
may create revolution.
Starting brings good fortune. No
blame.

Nine in the third place means:
Starting brings misfortune.
Perseverance brings danger.
When talk of revolution has gone
the rounds three times,
One may commit himself,
And men will believe him.

Nine in the fourth place means:
Remorse disappears. Men believe
him.
Changing the form of government
brings good fortune.

Nine in the fifth place means:
The great man changes like a tiger.
Even before he questions the oracle
He is believed.

Six at the top means:
The superior man changes like a
panther.
The inferior man molts in the face.
Starting brings misfortune.
To remain persevering brings good
fortune.

50

ting

above Li
The Clinging,
Flame

below Sun
The Gentle,
Wind

50. TING
The Caldron

THE JUDGEMENT

The Caldron. Supreme good
fortune.
Success.

THE IMAGE

Fire over wood:
The image of the Caldron.
Thus the superior man
consolidates his fate
By making his position correct.

THE LINES

Six at the beginning means:
A ting with legs upturned.
Furthers removal of stagnating stuff.
One takes a concubine for the sake
of her son.
No blame.

Nine in the second place means:
There is food in the ting.
My comrades are envious,
But they cannot harm me.
Good fortune.

Nine in the third place means:
The handle of the ting is altered.
One is impeded in his way of life.
The fat of the pheasant is not eaten.
Once rain falls, remorse is spent.
Good fortune comes in the end.

Nine in the fourth place means:
The legs of the ting are broken.
The prince's meal is spilled
And his person is soiled.
Misfortune.

Six in the fifth place means:
The ting has yellow handles, golden
carrying rings.
Perseverance furthers.

Nine at the top means:
The ting has rings of jade.
Great good fortune.
Nothing that would not act to
further.

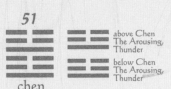

_51_

above Chen
The Arousing,
Thunder

below Chen
The Arousing,
Thunder

chen

51. CHEN
The Arousing (Shock, Thunder)

THE JUDGEMENT

Shock brings success.
Shock comes-oh, oh!
Laughing words-ha, ha!
The shock terrifies for a hundred
miles,
And he does not let fall the
sacrificial spoon and chalice.

THE IMAGE

Thunder repeated: the image of
Shock.
Thus in fear and trembling
The superior man sets his life in
order
And examines himself.

THE LINES

Nine at the beginning means:
Shock comes-oh, oh!
Then follow laughing words-ha, ha!
Good fortune.

Six in the second place means:
Shock comes bringing danger.
A hundred thousand times
You lose your treasures
And must climb the nine hills.
Do not go in pursuit of them.
After seven days you will get them
back.

Six in the third place means:
Shock comes and makes one
distraught.
If shock spurs to action
One remains free of misfortune.

Nine in the fourth place means:
Shock is mired.

Six in the fifth place means:
Shock goes hither and thither.
Danger.
However, nothing at all is lost.
Yet there are things to be done.

Six at the top means:
Shock brings ruin and terrified
gazing around.
Going ahead brings misfortune.
If it has not yet touched one's own
body
But has reached one's neighbor
first,
There is no blame.
One's comrades have something to
talk about.

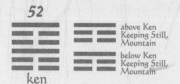

above Ken
Keeping Still,
Mountain

below Ken
Keeping Still,
Mountain

ken

52. KEN
Keeping Still, Mountain

THE JUDGEMENT

Keeping Still. Keeping his back still
So that he no longer feels his body.
He goes into his courtyard
And does not see his people.
No blame.

THE IMAGE

Mountains standing close together:
The image of Keeping Still.
Thus the superior man
Does not permit his thoughts
To go beyond his situation.

THE LINES

Six at the beginning means:
Keeping his toes still.
No blame.
Continued perseverance furthers.

Six in the second place means:
Keeping his calves still.
He cannot rescue him whom he
follows.
His heart is not glad.

Nine in the third place means:
Keeping his hips still.
Making his sacrum stiff.
Dangerous. The heart suffocates.

Six in the fourth place means:
Keeping his trunk still.
No blame.

Six in the fifth place means:
Keeping his jaws still.
The words have order.
Remorse disappears.

Nine at the top means:
Noblehearted keeping still.
Good fortune.

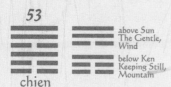

53

chien

above Sun
The Gentle,
Wind

below Ken
Keeping Still,
Mountain

53. CHIEN
Development (Gradual Progress)

THE JUDGEMENT

Development. The maiden
Is given in marriage.
Good fortune.
Perseverance furthers.

THE IMAGE

On the mountain, a tree:
The image of Development.
Thus the superior man abides in
dignity and virtue,
In order to improve the mores.

THE LINES

Six at the beginning means:
The wild goose gradually draws
near the shore.
The young son is in danger.
There is talk. No blame.

Six in the second place means:
The wild goose gradually draws
near the cliff.
Eating and drinking in peace and
concord.
Good fortune.

Nine in the third place means:
The wild goose gradually draws
near the plateau.
The man goes forth and does not
return.
The woman carries a child but does
not bring it forth.
Misfortune.
It furthers one to fight off robbers.

Six in the fourth place means:
The wild goose gradually draws
near the tree.
Perhaps it will find a flat branch.
No blame.

Nine in the fifth place means:
The wild goose gradually draws
near the summit.
For three years the woman has no
child.
In the end nothing can hinder her.
Good fortune.

Nine at the top means:
The wild goose gradually draws
near the cloud heights.
Its feathers can be used for the
sacred dance.
Good fortune.

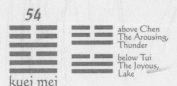

54

kuei mei

above Chen
The Arousing,
Thunder

below Tui
The Joyous,
Lake

54. KUEI MEI
The Marrying Maiden

THE JUDGEMENT

The Marrying Maiden.
Undertakings bring misfortune.
Nothing that would further.

THE IMAGE

Thunder over the lake:
The image of the Marrying Maiden.
Thus the superior man
Understands the transitory
In the light of the eternity of the
end.

THE LINES

Nine at the beginning means:
The marrying maiden as a
concubine.
A lame man who is able to tread.
Undertakings bring good fortune.

Nine in the second place means:
A one-eyed man who is able to see.
The perseverance of a solitary man
furthers.

Six in the third place means:
The marrying maiden as a slave.
She marries as a concubine.

Nine in the fourth place means:
The marrying maiden draws out the
allotted time.
A late marriage comes in due course.

Six in the fifth place means:
The sovereign I gave his daughter in
marriage.
The embroidered garments of the
princess
Were not as gorgeous
As those of the servingmaid.
The moon that is nearly full
Brings good fortune.

Six at the top means:
The woman holds the basket, but
there are no fruits in it.
The man stabs the sheep, but no
blood flows.
Nothing that acts to further.

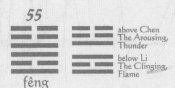

above Chen
The Arousing,
Thunder

below Li
The Clinging,
Flame

55. FENG
Abundance [Fullness]

THE JUDGEMENT

Abundance has success.
The king attains abundance.
Be not sad.
Be like the sun at midday.

THE IMAGE

Both thunder and lightning come:
The image of Abundance.
Thus the superior man decides lawsuits
And carries out punishments.

THE LINES

Nine at the beginning means:
When a man meets his destined ruler,
They can be together ten days,
And it is not a mistake.
Going meets with recognition.

Six in the second place means:
The curtain is of such fullness
That the polestars can be seen at noon.
Through going one meets with mistrust and hate.
If one rouses him through truth,
Good fortune comes.

Nine in the third place means:
The underbrush is of such abundance
That the small stars can be seen at noon.
He breaks his right arm. No blame.

Nine in the fourth place means:
The curtain is of such fullness
That the polestars can be seen at noon.
He meets his ruler, who is of like kind.
Good fortune.

Six in the fifth place means:
Lines are coming,
Blessing and fame draw near.
Good fortune.

Six at the top means:
His house is in a state of abundance.
He screens off his family.
He peers through the gate
And no longer perceives anyone.
For three years he sees nothing.
Misfortune.

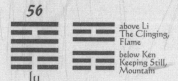

56

above Li
The Clinging,
Flame

below Ken
Keeping Still,
Mountain

56. LU
The Wanderer

THE JUDGEMENT

The Wanderer. Success through
smallness.
Perseverance brings good fortune
To the wanderer.

THE IMAGE

Fire on the mountain:
The image of the Wanderer.
Thus the superior man
Is clear-minded and cautious
In imposing penalties,
And protracts no lawsuits.

THE LINES

Six at the beginning means:
If the wanderer busies himself with
trivial things,
He draws down misfortune upon
himself.

Six in the second place means:
The wanderer comes to an inn.
He has his property with him.
He wins the steadfastness of a
young servant.

Nine in the third place means:
The wanderer's inn burns down.
He loses the steadfastness of his
young servant.
Danger.

Nine in the fourth place means:
The wanderer rests in a shelter.
He obtains his property and an ox.
My heart is not glad.

Six in the fifth place means:
He shoots a pheasant.
It drops with the first arrow.
In the end this brings both praise
and office.

Nine at the top means:
The bird's nest burns up.
The wanderer laughs at first,
Then must needs lament and weep.
Through carelessness he loses his
cow.
Misfortune.

above Sun
The Gentle,
Wind

below Sun
The Gentle,
Wind

sun

57. SUN
The Gentle

THE JUDGEMENT

The Gentle. Success through what
is small.
It furthers one to have somewhere
to go.
It furthers one to see the great man.

THE IMAGE

Winds following one upon the
other:
The image of the Gently
Penetrating.
Thus the superior man
Spreads his commands abroad
And carries out his undertakings.

THE LINES

Six at the beginning means:
In advancing and in retreating,
The perseverance of a warrior
furthers.

Nine in the second place means:
Penetration under the bed.
Priests and magicians are used in
great number.
Good fortune. No blame.

Nine in the third place means:
Repeated penetration. Humiliation.

Six in the fourth place means:
Remorse vanishes.
During the hunt
Three kinds of game are caught.

Nine in the fifth place means:
Perseverance brings good fortune.
Remorse vanishes.
Nothing that does not further.
No beginning, but an end.
Before the change, three days.
After the change, three days.
Good fortune.

Nine at the top means:
Penetration under the bed.
He loses his property and his ax.
Perseverance brings misfortune.

58

above Tui
The Joyous,
Lake

below Tui
The Joyous,
Lake

tui

58. TUI
The Joyous, Lake

THE JUDGEMENT

The Joyous. Success.
Perseverance is favourable.

THE IMAGE

Lakes resting one on the other:
The image of the Joyous.
Thus the superior man joins with his friends
For discussion and practice.

THE LINES

Nine at the beginning means:
Contented joyousness. Good fortune.

Nine in the second place means:
Sincere joyousness. Good fortune.
Remorse disappears.

Six in the third place means:
Coming joyousness. Misfortune.

Nine in the fourth place means:
Joyousness that is weighed is not at peace.
After ridding himself of mistakes a man has joy.

Nine in the fifth place means:
Sincerity toward disintegrating influences is dangerous.

Six at the top means:
Seductive joyousness.

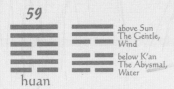

59

huan

above Sun
The Gentle,
Wind

below K'an
The Abysmal,
Water

59. HUAN
Dispersion [Dissolution]

THE JUDGEMENT

Dispersion. Success.
The king approaches his temple.
It furthers one to cross the great
water.
Perseverance furthers.

THE IMAGE

The wind drives over the water:
The image of Dispersion.
Thus the kings of old sacrificed to
the Lord
And built temples.

THE LINES

Six at the beginning means:
He brings help with the strength of
a horse.
Good fortune.

Nine in the second place means:
At the dissolution
He hurries to that which supports
him.
Remorse disappears.

Six in the third place means:
He dissolves his self. No remorse.

Six in the fourth place means:
He dissolves his bond with his
group.
Supreme good fortune.
Dispersion leads in turn to
accumulation.
This is something that ordinary
men do not think of.

Nine in the fifth place means:
His loud cries are as dissolving as
sweat.
Dissolution. A king abides without
blame.

Nine at the top means:
He dissolves his blood.
Departing, keeping at a distance,
going out,
Is without blame.

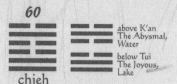

60

above K'an
The Abysmal,
Water

below Tui
The Joyous,
Lake

chieh

60. CHIEH
Limitation

THE JUDGEMENT

Limitation. Success.
Galling limitation must not be
persevered in.

THE IMAGE

Water over lake: the image of
Limitation.
Thus the superior man
Creates number and measure,
And examines the nature of virtue
and correct conduct.

THE LINES

Nine at the beginning means:
Not going out of the door and the
courtyard
Is without blame.

Nine in the second place means:
Not going out of the gate and the
courtyard
Brings misfortune.

Six in the third place means:
He who knows no limitation
Will have cause to lament.
No blame.

Six in the fourth place means:
Contented limitation. Success.

Nine in the fifth place means:
Sweet limitation brings good
fortune.
Going brings esteem.

Six at the top means:
Galling limitation.
Perseverance brings misfortune.
Remorse disappears.

chung fu

above Sun
The Gentle,
Wind

below Tui
The Joyous,
Lake

61. CHUNG FU
Inner Truth

THE JUDGEMENT

Inner Truth. Pigs and fishes.
Good fortune.
It furthers one to cross the great
water.
Perseverance furthers.

THE IMAGE

Wind over lake: the image of Inner
Truth.
Thus the superior man discusses
criminal cases
In order to delay executions.

THE LINES

Nine at the beginning means:
Being prepared brings good fortune.
If there are secret designs, it is
disquieting.

Nine in the second place means:
A crane calling in the shade.
Its young answers it.
I have a good goblet.
I will share it with you.

Six in the third place means:
He finds a comrade.
Now he beats the drum, now he
stops.
Now he sobs, now he sings.

Six in the fourth place means:
The moon nearly at the full.
The team horse goes astray.
No blame.

Nine in the fifth place means:
He possesses truth, which links
together.
No blame.

Nine at the top means:
Cockcrow penetrating to heaven.
Perseverance brings misfortune.

62

hsiao kuo

above Chen
The Arousing,
Thunder

below Ken
Keeping Still,
Mountain

62. Hsiao Kuo
Preponderance of the Small

The Judgement

Preponderance of the Small.
Success.
Perseverance furthers.
Small things may be done; great
things should not be done.
The flying bird brings the message:
It is not well to strive upward,
It is well to remain below.
Great good fortune.

The Image

Thunder on the mountain:
The image of Preponderance of the
Small.
Thus in his conduct the superior
man gives preponderance to
reverence.
In bereavement he gives
preponderance to grief.
In his expenditures he gives
preponderance to thrift.

The Lines

The Lines
Six at the beginning means:
The bird meets with misfortune
through flying.

Six in the second place means:
She passes by her ancestor
And meets her ancestress.
He does not reach his prince
And meets the official.
No blame.

Nine in the third place means:
If one is not extremely careful,
Somebody may come up from behind
and strike him.
Misfortune.

Nine in the fourth place means:
No blame. He meets him without
passing by.
Going brings danger. One must be
on guard.
Do not act. Be constantly
persevering.

Six in the fifth place means:
Dense clouds,
No rain from our western territory.
The prince shoots and hits him who
is in the cave.

Six at the top means:
He passes him by, not meeting him.
The flying bird leaves him.
Misfortune.
This means bad luck and injury.

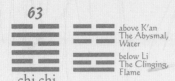

above K'an
The Abysmal,
Water

below Li
The Clinging,
Flame

chi chi

63. CHI CHI
After Completion

THE JUDGEMENT

After Completion. Success in small
matters.
Perseverance furthers.
At the beginning good fortune,
At the end disorder.

THE IMAGE

Water over fire: the image of the
condition
In After Completion.
Thus the superior man
Takes thought of misfortune
And arms himself against it in
advance.

THE LINES

Nine at the beginning means:
He brakes his wheels.
He gets his tail in the water.
No blame.

Six in the second place means:
The woman loses the curtain of her
carriage.
Do not run after it;
On the seventh day you will get it.

Nine in the third place means:
The Illustrious Ancestor
Disciplines the Devil's Country.
After three years he conquers it.
Inferior people must not be
employed.

Six in the fourth place means:
The finest clothes turn to rags.
Be careful all day long.

Nine in the fifth place means:
The neighbor in the east who
slaughters an ox
Does not attain as much real
happiness
As the neighbor in the west
With his small offering.

Six at the top means:
He gets his head in the water.
Danger.

wei chi

above Li
The Clinging,
Flame

below K'an
The Abysmal,
Water

64. WEI CHI
Before Completion

THE JUDGEMENT

Before Completion. Success.
But if the little fox, after nearly
completing the crossing,
Gets his tail in the water,
There is nothing that would further.

THE IMAGE

Fire over water:
The image of the condition before
transition.
Thus the superior man is careful
In the differentiation of things,
So that each finds its place.

THE LINES

Six at the beginning means:
He gets his tail in the water.
Humiliating.

Nine in the second place means:
He brakes his wheels.
Perseverance brings good fortune.

Six in the third place means:
Before completion, attack brings
misfortune.
It furthers one to cross the great
water.

Nine in the fourth place means:
Perseverance brings good fortune.
Remorse disappears.
Shock, thus to discipline the Devil's
Country.
For three years, great realms are
awarded.

Six in the fifth place means:
Perseverance brings good fortune.
No remorse.
The light of the superior man is true.
Good fortune.

Nine at the top means:
There is drinking of wine
In genuine confidence. No blame.
But if one wets his head,
He loses it, in truth.

Hexagram Record Keeper

The taiji symbol seen throughout Taoist and Asian Philosophy represents the balance of polarities of the yin/yang interplay of 'chi' energy

Chinese symbol of balance, luck and harmony

The dragon, a renown symbol of strength, goodness, and fertility

The crane is symbolic of longevity and good health